MANHATTAN PREP

Algebra

GRE® Strategy Guide

This essential guide covers algebra in all its various forms (and disguises) on the GRE. Master fundamental techniques and nuanced strategies to help you solve for unknown variables of every type.

guide **1**

Algebra GRE Strategy Guide, Fourth Edition

10-digit International Standard Book Number: 1-937707-83-0
13-digit International Standard Book Number: 978-1-937707-83-5
eISBN: 978-1-941234-13-6

Note: *GRE, Graduate Record Exam, Educational Testing Service,* and *ETS* are all registered trademarks of the Educational Testing Service, which neither sponsors nor is affiliated in any way with this product.

Layout Design: Dan McNaney and Cathy Huang
Cover Design: Dan McNaney and Frank Callaghan
Cover Photography: Sam Edla

INSTRUCTIONAL GUIDE SERIES

SUPPLEMENTAL MATERIALS

MANHATTAN
PREP

June 3rd, 2014

Dear Student,

Thank you for picking up a copy of GRE *Algebra*. I hope this book provides just the guidance you need to get the most out of your GRE studies.

As with most accomplishments, there were many people involved in the creation of the book you are holding. First and foremost is Zeke Vanderhoek, the founder of Manhattan Prep. Zeke was a lone tutor in New York when he started the company in 2000. Now, 14 years later, the company has instructors and offices nationwide and contributes to the studies and successes of thousands of GRE, GMAT, LSAT, and SAT students each year.

Our Manhattan Prep Strategy Guides are based on the continuing experiences of our instructors and students. We are particularly indebted to our instructors Stacey Koprince, Dave Mahler, Liz Ghini Moliski, Emily Meredith Sledge, and Tommy Wallach for their hard work on this edition. Dan McNaney and Cathy Huang provided their design expertise to make the books as user-friendly as possible, and Liz Krisher made sure all the moving pieces came together at just the right time. Beyond providing additions and edits for this book, Chris Ryan and Noah Teitelbaum continue to be the driving force behind all of our curriculum efforts. Their leadership is invaluable. Finally, thank you to all of the Manhattan Prep students who have provided input and feedback over the years. This book wouldn't be half of what it is without your voice.

At Manhattan Prep, we continually aspire to provide the best instructors and resources possible. We hope that you will find our commitment manifest in this book. If you have any questions or comments, please email me at dgonzalez@manhattanprep.com. I'll look forward to reading your comments, and I'll be sure to pass them along to our curriculum team.

Thanks again, and best of luck preparing for the GRE!

Sincerely,

Dan Gonzalez
President
Manhattan Prep

HOW TO ACCESS YOUR ONLINE RESOURCES

If you...

⊙ **are a registered Manhattan Prep GRE® student**

and have received this book as part of your course materials, you have AUTOMATIC access to ALL of our online resources. This includes all practice exams, question banks, and online updates to this book. To access these resources, follow the instructions in the Welcome Guide provided to you at the start of your program. Do NOT follow the instructions below.

⊙ **purchased this book from the Manhattan Prep online store or at one of our centers**

1. Go to: www.manhattanprep.com/gre/studentcenter.

2. Log in using the username and password used when your account was set up.

⊙ **purchased this book at a retail location**

1. Create an account with Manhattan Prep at the website: www.manhattanprep.com/gre/createaccount.

2. Go to: www.manhattanprep.com/gre/access.

3. Follow the instructions on the screen.

Your online access begins on the day that you register your book at the above URL.

You only need to register your product ONCE at the above URL. To use your online resources any time AFTER you have completed the registration process, log in to the following URL: www.manhattanprep.com/gre/studentcenter.

Please note that online access is nontransferable. This means that only NEW and UNREGISTERED copies of the book will grant you online access. Previously used books will NOT provide any online resources.

⊙ **purchased an eBook version of this book**

1. Create an account with Manhattan Prep at the website: www.manhattanprep.com/gre/createaccount.

2. Email a copy of your purchase receipt to gre@manhattanprep.com to activate your resources. Please be sure to use the same email address to create an account that you used to purchase the eBook.

For any technical issues, email techsupport@manhattanprep.com or call 800-576-4628.

TABLE *of* CONTENTS

guide **1**

Chapter 1

of

Algebra

Introduction

In This Chapter...

The Revised GRE

Question Formats in Detail

Chapter 1

Introduction

We know that you're looking to succeed on the GRE so that you can go to graduate school and do the things you want to do in life.

We also know that you may not have done math since high school, and that you may never have learned words like "adumbrate" or "sangfroid." We know that it's going to take hard work on your part to get a top GRE score, and that's why we've put together the only set of books that will take you from the basics all the way up to the material you need to master for a near-perfect score, or whatever your goal score may be. You've taken the first step. Now it's time to get to work!

How to Use These Materials

Manhattan Prep's GRE materials are comprehensive. But keep in mind that, depending on your score goal, it may not be necessary to get absolutely everything. Grad schools only see your overall Quantitative, Verbal, and Writing scores—they don't see exactly which strengths and weaknesses went into creating those scores.

You may be enrolled in one of our courses, in which case you already have a syllabus telling you in what order you should approach the books. But if you bought this book online or at a bookstore, feel free to approach the books—and even the chapters within the books—in whatever order works best for you. For the most part, the books, and the chapters within them, are independent; you don't have to master one section before moving on to the next. So if you're having a hard time with something in particular, you can make a note to come back to it later and move on to another section. Similarly, it may not be necessary to solve every single practice problem for every section. As you go through the material, continually assess whether you understand and can apply the principles in each individual section and chapter. The best way to do this is to solve the Check Your Skills and Practice Sets throughout. If you're confident you have a concept or method down, feel free to move on. If you struggle with something, make note of it for further review. Stay active in your learning and stay oriented toward the test—it's easy to read something and think you understand it, only to have trouble applying it in the 1–2 minutes you have to solve a problem.

1

Study Skills

As you're studying for the GRE, try to integrate your learning into your everyday life. For example, vocabulary is a big part of the GRE, as well as something you just can't "cram" for—you're going to want to do at least a little bit of vocab every day. So try to learn and internalize a little bit at a time, switching up topics often to help keep things interesting.

Keep in mind that, while many of your study materials are on paper (including Education Testing Service's [ETS's] most recent source of official GRE questions, *The Official Guide to the GRE revised General Test, Second Edition*), your exam will be administered on a computer. Because this is a computer-based test, you will *not* be able to underline portions of reading passages, write on diagrams of geometry figures, or otherwise physically mark up problems. So get used to this now. Solve the problems in these books on scratch paper. (Each of our books talks specifically about what to write down for different problem types.)

Again, as you study, stay focused on the test-day experience. As you progress, work on timed drills and sets of questions. Eventually, you should be taking full practice tests (available at www.manhattanprep.com/gre) under actual timed conditions.

The Revised GRE

As of August 1, 2011, the Quantitative and Verbal sections of the GRE underwent a number of changes. The actual body of knowledge being tested is more or less the same as it ever was, but the *way* that knowledge is tested changed. Here's a brief summary of the changes, followed by a more comprehensive assessment of the new exam.

The current test is a little longer than the old test, lengthened from about 3.5 hours to about 4 hours. When you sign up for the exam at www.ets.org/gre, you will be told to plan to be at the center for 5 hours, since there will be some paperwork to complete when you arrive, and occasionally test-takers are made to wait a bit before being allowed to begin.

Taking a four-hour exam can be quite exhausting, so it's important to practice not only out of these books, but also on full-length computer-based practice exams, such as the six such exams you have gained access to by purchasing this book (see page 7 for details).

There are now two scored Math sections and two scored Verbal sections. A new score scale of 130–170 is used in place of the old 200–800 scale. More on this later.

The Verbal section of the GRE changed dramatically. The Antonyms and Analogies disappeared. The Text Completion and Reading Comprehension remain, expanded and remixed in a few new ways. Vocabulary is still important, but is tested only in the context of complete sentences.

1

The Quant section of the new GRE still contains the same multiple-choice problems, Quantitative Comparisons, and Data Interpretations (which are really a subset of multiple-choice problems). The revised test also contains two new problem formats, which we will introduce in this section.

On both Verbal and Quant, some of the new question types have more than one correct answer, or otherwise break out of the mold of traditional multiple-choice exams. You might say that computer-based exams are finally taking advantage of the features of computers.

One way that this is true is that the new exam includes a small, on-screen, four-function calculator with a square root button. Many test-takers will rejoice at the advent of this calculator. It is true that the GRE calculator will reduce emphasis on computation—but look out for problems, such as percents questions with tricky wording, that are likely to foil those who rely on the calculator too much. *In short, the calculator may make your life a bit easier from time to time, but it's not a game changer.* There are **zero** questions that can be solved *entirely* with a calculator. You will still need to know the principles contained in the six Quant books (of the eight-book Manhattan Prep GRE series).

Finally, don't worry about whether the new GRE is harder or easier than the old GRE. You are being judged against other test-takers, all of whom are in the same boat. So if the new formats are harder, they are harder for other test-takers as well.

Additionally, graduate schools to which you will be applying have been provided with conversion charts so that applicants with old and new GRE scores can be compared fairly (GRE scores are valid for five years).

Exam Structure

The revised test has six sections. You will get a 10-minute break between the third and fourth sections and a 1-minute break between the others. The Analytical Writing section is always first. The other five sections can be seen in any order and will include:

- Two Verbal Reasoning sections (20 questions each in 30 minutes per section)
- Two Quantitative Reasoning sections (20 questions each in 35 minutes per section)
- Either an unscored section or a research section

An unscored section will look just like a third Verbal or Quantitative Reasoning section, and you will not be told which of them doesn't count. If you get a research section, it will be identified as such, and will be the last section you get.

Section #	Section Type	# Questions	Time	Scored?
1	Analytical Writing	2 essays	30 minutes each	Yes
2	Verbal #1	Approx. 20	30 minutes	Yes
3	Quantitative #1 *(order can vary)*	Approx. 20	35 minutes	Yes
10-Minute Break				
4	Verbal #2	Approx. 20	30 minutes	Yes
5	Quantitative #2 *(order can vary)*	Approx. 20	35 minutes	Yes
?	Unscored Section *(Verbal or Quant, order can vary)*	Approx. 20	30 or 35 minutes	No
Last	Research Section	Varies	Varies	No

All the question formats will be looked at in detail later in the chapter.

Using the Calculator

The addition of a small, four-function calculator with a square root button means that re-memorizing times tables or square roots is less important than it used to be. However, the calculator is not a cure-all; in many problems, the difficulty is in figuring out what numbers to put into the calculator in the first place. In some cases, using a calculator will actually be less helpful than doing the problem some other way. Take a look at an example:

> If x is the remainder when (11)(7) is divided by 4 and y is the remainder when (14)
> (6) is divided by 13, what is the value of $x + y$?

Solution: This problem is designed so that the calculator won't tell the whole story. Certainly, the calculator will tell you that $11 \times 7 = 77$. When you divide 77 by 4, however, the calculator yields an answer of 19.25. The remainder is not 0.25 (a remainder is always a whole number).

You might just go back to your pencil and paper, and find the largest multiple of 4 that is less than 77. Since 4 does go into 76, you can conclude that 4 would leave a remainder of 1 when dividing into 77.

1

(Notice that you don't even need to know how many times 4 goes into 76, just that it goes in. One way to mentally "jump" to 76 is to say, 4 goes into 40, so it goes into 80…that's a bit too big, so take away 4 to get 76.)

However, it is also possible to use the calculator to find a remainder. Divide 77 by 4 to get 19.25. Thus, 4 goes into 77 nineteen times, with a remainder left over. Now use your calculator to multiply 19 (JUST 19, not 19.25) by 4. You will get 76. The remainder is $77 - 76$, which is 1. Therefore, $x = 1$. You could also multiply the leftover 0.25 times 4 (the divisor) to find the remainder of 1.

Use the same technique to find y. Multiply 14 by 6 to get 84. Divide 84 by 13 to get 6.46. Ignore everything after the decimal, and just multiply 6 by 13 to get 78. The remainder is therefore $84 - 78$, which is 6. Therefore, $y = 6$.

Since you are looking for $x + y$, and $1 + 6 = 7$, the answer is 7.

You can see that blind faith in the calculator can be dangerous. Use it responsibly! And this leads us to…

Practice Using the Calculator!

On the revised GRE, the on-screen calculator will slow you down or lead to incorrect answers if you're not careful! If you plan to use it on test day (which you should), you'll want to practice first.

We have created an online practice calculator for you to use. To access this calculator, go to **www.manhattanprep.com/gre** and sign in to the student center using the instructions on the "How to Access Your Online Resources" page found at the front of this book.

In addition to the calculator, you will see instructions for how to use the calculator. Be sure to read these instructions and work through the associated exercises. Throughout our math books, you will see the [calculator] symbol. This symbol means "Use the calculator here!" As much as possible, have the online practice calculator up and running during your review of our math books. You'll have the chance to use the on-screen calculator when you take our practice exams as well.

Navigating the Questions in a Section

Another change for test-takers on the revised GRE is the ability to move freely around the questions in a section—you can go forward and backward one-by-one and can even jump directly to any question from the "review list." The review list provides a snapshot of which questions you have answered, which ones you have tagged for "mark and review," and which are incomplete, either because you didn't indicate enough answers or because you indicated too many (that is, if a number of choices is specified by the question). You should double-check the review list for completion if you finish the section early. Using the review list feature will take some practice as well, which is why we've built it into our online practice exams.

1

The majority of test-takers will be pressed for time. Thus, for some, it won't be feasible to go back to multiple problems at the end of the section. Generally, if you can't get a question the first time, you won't be able to get it the second time around either. With this in mind, here's the order in which we recommend using the new review list feature.

1. Do the questions in the order in which they appear.

2. When you encounter a difficult question, do your best to eliminate answer choices you know are wrong.

3. If you're not sure of an answer, take an educated guess from the choices remaining. Do NOT skip it and hope to return to it later.

4. Using the "mark" button at the top of the screen, mark up to three questions per section that you think you might be able to solve with more time. Mark a question only after you have taken an educated guess.

5. Always click on the review list at the end of a section, to quickly make sure you have neither skipped nor incompletely answered any questions.

6. If you have time, identify any questions that you marked for review and return to them. If you do not have any time remaining, you will have already taken good guesses at the tough ones.

What you want to avoid is surfing—clicking forward and backward through the questions searching for the easy ones. This will eat up valuable time. Of course, you'll want to move through the tough ones quickly if you can't get them, but try to avoid skipping around.

Again, all of this will take practice. Use our practice exams to fine-tune your approach.

Scoring

You need to know two things about the scoring of the revised GRE Verbal Reasoning and Quantitative Reasoning sections: (1) how individual questions influence the score, and (2) the score scale itself.

For both the Verbal Reasoning and Quantitative Reasoning sections, you will receive a scaled score, based on both how many questions you answered correctly and the difficulties of the specific questions you actually saw.

The old GRE was question-adaptive, meaning that your answer to each question (right or wrong) determined, at least somewhat, the questions that followed (harder or easier). Because you had to commit to an answer to let the algorithm do its thing, you weren't allowed to skip questions or to go back to change answers. On the revised GRE, the adapting occurs from section to section rather than from question to question (e.g., if you do well on the first Verbal section, you will get a harder second Verbal section). The only change test-takers will notice is one that most will welcome: you can now move freely about the questions in a section, coming back to tough questions later, changing answers after "Aha!" moments, and generally managing your time more flexibly.

The scores for the revised GRE Quantitative Reasoning and Verbal Reasoning are reported on a 130–170 scale in 1-point increments, whereas the old score reporting was on a 200–800 scale in 10-point increments. You will receive one 130–170 score for Verbal and a separate 130–170 score for Quant. If you are already putting your GRE math skills to work, you may notice that there are now 41 scores possible (170 − 130, then add 1 before you're done), whereas before there were 61 scores possible ([800 − 200]/10, then add 1 before you're done). In other words, a 10-point difference on the old score scale actually indicated a smaller performance differential than a 1-point difference on the new scale. However, the GRE folks argue that perception is reality: the difference between 520 and 530 on the old scale could simply seem greater than the difference between 151 and 152 on the new scale. If that's true, then this change will benefit test-takers, who won't be unfairly compared by schools for minor differences in performance. If not true, then the change is moot.

Question Formats in Detail

Essay Questions

The Analytical Writing section consists of two separately timed 30-minute tasks: Analyze an Issue and Analyze an Argument. As you can imagine, the 30-minute time limit implies that you aren't aiming to write an essay that would garner a Pulitzer Prize nomination, but rather to complete the tasks adequately and according to the directions. Each essay is scored separately, but your reported essay score is the average of the two, rounded up to the next half-point increment on a 0–6 scale.

Issue Task: This essay prompt will present a claim, generally one that is vague enough to be interpreted in various ways and discussed from numerous perspectives. Your job as a test-taker is to write a response discussing the extent to which you agree or disagree and support your position. Don't sit on the fence—pick a side!

For some examples of Issue Task prompts, visit the GRE website here:

> www.ets.org/gre/revised_general/prepare/analytical_writing/issue/pool

Argument Task: This essay prompt will be an argument comprised of both a claim (or claims) and evidence. Your job is to dispassionately discuss the argument's structural flaws and merits (well, mostly the flaws). Don't agree or disagree with the argument—simply evaluate its logic.

For some examples of Argument Task prompts, visit the GRE website here:

> www.ets.org/gre/revised_general/prepare/analytical_writing/argument/pool

Verbal: Reading Comprehension Questions

Standard five-choice multiple-choice Reading Comprehension questions continue to appear on the revised exam. You are likely familiar with how these work. Let's take a look at two *new* Reading Comprehension formats that will appear on the revised test.

Select One or More Answer Choices and Select-in-Passage

For the question type "Select One or More Answer Choices," you are given three statements about a passage and asked to "indicate all that apply." Either one, two, or all three can be correct (there is no "none of the above" option). There is no partial credit; you must indicate all of the correct choices and none of the incorrect choices.

Strategy Tip: On "Select One or More Answer Choices," don't let your brain be tricked into telling you, "Well, if two of them have been right so far, the other one must be wrong," or any other arbitrary idea about how many of the choices *should* be correct. Make sure to consider each choice independently! You cannot use "process of elimination" in the same way as you do on normal multiple-choice questions.

For the question type "Select-in-Passage," you are given an assignment such as "Select the sentence in the passage that explains why the experiment's results were discovered to be invalid." Clicking anywhere on the sentence in the passage will highlight it. (As with any GRE question, you will have to click "Confirm" to submit your answer, so don't worry about accidentally selecting the wrong sentence due to a slip of the mouse.)

Strategy Tip: On "Select-in-Passage," if the passage is short, consider numbering each sentence (i.e., writing 1 2 3 4 on your paper) and crossing off each choice as you determine that it isn't the answer. If the passage is long, you might write a number for each paragraph (I, II, III), and tick off each number as you determine that the correct sentence is not located in that paragraph.

Now give these new question types a try:

The sample questions below are based on this passage:

> Physicist Robert Oppenheimer, director of the fateful Manhattan Project, said, "It is a profound and necessary truth that the deep things in science are not found because they are useful; they are found because it was possible to find them." In a later address at MIT, Oppenheimer presented the thesis that scientists could be held only very nominally responsible for the consequences of their research and discovery. Oppenheimer asserted that ethics, philosophy, and politics have very little to do with the day-to-day work of the scientist, and that scientists could not rationally be expected to predict all the effects of their work. Yet, in a talk in 1945 to the Association of Los Alamos Scientists, Oppenheimer offered some reasons why the Manhattan Project scientists built the atomic bomb; the justifications included "fear that Nazi Germany would build it first" and "hope that it would shorten the war."

For question #1, consider each of the three choices separately and indicate all that apply.

1. The passage implies that Robert Oppenheimer would most likely have agreed with which of the following views:

   [A] Some scientists take military goals into account in their work
   [B] Deep things in science are not useful
   [C] The everyday work of a scientist is only minimally involved with ethics

2. Select the sentence in which the writer implies that Oppenheimer has not been consistent in his view that scientists have little consideration for the effects of their work.

(Here, you would highlight the appropriate sentence with your mouse. Note that there are only four options.)

Solutions

1. **(A)** and **(C):** Oppenheimer says in the last sentence that one of the reasons the bomb was built was scientists' *hope that it would shorten the war.* Thus, Oppenheimer would likely agree with the view that *Some scientists take military goals into account in their work.* (B) is a trap answer using familiar language from the passage. Oppenheimer says that scientific discoveries' possible usefulness is not why scientists make discoveries; he does not say that the discoveries aren't useful. Oppenheimer specifically says that ethics has *very little to do with the day-to-day work of the scientist*, which is a good match for *only minimally involved with ethics.*

Strategy Tip: On "Select One or More Answer Choices," write A B C on your paper and mark each choice with a check, an *X*, or a symbol such as ~ if you're not sure. This should keep you from crossing out all three choices and having to go back (at least one of the choices must be correct). For example, say that on a *different* question you had marked

   A. *X*
   B. ~
   C. *X*

The answer choice you weren't sure about, (B), is likely to be correct, since there must be at least one correct answer.

---

2. The correct sentence is: **Yet, in a talk in 1945 to the Association of Los Alamos Scientists, Oppenheimer offered some reasons why the Manhattan Project scientists built the atomic bomb; the justifications included "fear that Nazi Germany would build it first" and "hope that it would shorten the war."** The word "yet" is a good clue that this sentence is about to express a view contrary to the views expressed in the rest of the passage.

Verbal: Text Completion Questions

Text Completions can consist of 1–5 sentences with 1–3 blanks. When Text Completions have two or three blanks, you will select words or short phrases for those blanks independently. There is no partial credit; you must make every selection correctly.

> Leaders are not always expected to (i) _____ the same rules as are
> those they lead; leaders are often looked up to for a surety and presumption that
> would be viewed as (ii) _____ in most others.

Blank (i)	Blank (ii)
decree	hubris
proscribe	avarice
conform to	anachronism

Select your two choices by actually clicking and highlighting the words you want.

Solution

In the first blank, you need a word similar to "follow." In the second blank, you need a word similar to "arrogance." The correct answers are *conform to* and *hubris*.

Strategy Tip: Do NOT look at the answer choices until you've decided for yourself, based on textual clues actually written in the sentence, what kind of word needs to go in each blank. Only then should you look at the choices and eliminate those that are not matches.

Now try an example with three blanks:

> For Kant, the fact of having a right and having the (i) _____ to enforce it
> via coercion cannot be separated, and he asserts that this marriage of rights and
> coercion is compatible with the freedom of everyone. This is not at all peculiar
> from the standpoint of modern political thought—what good is a right if its violation
> triggers no enforcement (be it punishment or (ii) _____)? The necessity
> of coercion is not at all in conflict with the freedom of everyone, because this
> coercion only comes into play when someone has (iii) _____ someone else.

Blank (i)	Blank (ii)	Blank (iii)
technique	amortization	questioned the hypothesis of
license	reward	violated the rights of
prohibition	restitution	granted civil liberties to

1

Solution

In the first sentence, use the clue "he asserts that this marriage of rights and coercion is compatible with the freedom of everyone" to help fill in the first blank. Kant believes that "coercion" is "married to" rights and is compatible with freedom for all. So you want something in the first blank like "right" or "power." Kant believes that rights are meaningless without enforcement. Only the choice *license* can work (while a *license* can be physical, like a driver's license, *license* can also mean "right").

The second blank is part of the phrase "punishment or _____," which you are told is the "enforcement" resulting from the violation of a right. So the blank should be something, other than punishment, that constitutes enforcement against someone who violates a right. (More simply, it should be something bad.) Only *restitution* works. Restitution is compensating the victim in some way (perhaps monetarily or by returning stolen goods).

In the final sentence, "coercion only comes into play when someone has _____ someone else." Throughout the text, "coercion" means enforcement against someone who has violated the rights of someone else. The meaning is the same here. The answer is *violated the rights of.*

The complete and correct answer is this combination:

Blank (i)	Blank (ii)	Blank (iii)
license	restitution	violated the rights of

In theory, there are 3 × 3 × 3, or 27 possible ways to answer a three-blank Text Completion—and only one of those 27 ways is correct. In theory, these are bad odds. In practice, you will often have certainty about some of the blanks, so your guessing odds are almost never this bad. Just follow the basic process: come up with your own filler for each blank, and match to the answer choices. If you're confused by this example, don't worry! The Manhattan Prep *Text Completion & Sentence Equivalence GRE Strategy Guide* covers all of this in detail.

Strategy Tip: Do not write your own story. The GRE cannot give you a blank without also giving you a clue, physically written down in the passage, telling you what kind of word or phrase must go in that blank. Find that clue. You should be able to give textual evidence for each answer choice you select.

Verbal: Sentence Equivalence Questions

For this question type, you are given one sentence with a single blank. There are six answer choices, and you are asked to pick two choices that fit the blank and are alike in meaning.

Of the Verbal question types, this one depends the most on vocabulary and also yields the most to strategy.

1

No partial credit is given on Sentence Equivalence; both correct answers must be selected and no incorrect answers may be selected. When you pick 2 of 6 choices, there are 15 possible combinations of choices, and only one is correct. However, this is not nearly as daunting as it sounds.

Think of it this way: if you have six choices, but the two correct ones must be similar in meaning, then you have, at most, three possible *pairs* of choices, maybe fewer, since not all choices are guaranteed to have a partner. If you can match up the pairs, you can seriously narrow down your options.

Here is a sample set of answer choices:

> A　tractable
> B　taciturn
> C　arbitrary
> D　tantamount
> E　reticent
> F　amenable

The question is deliberately omitted here in order to illustrate how much you can do with the choices alone, if you have studied vocabulary sufficiently.

Tractable and *amenable* are synonyms (tractable, amenable people will do whatever you want them to do). *Taciturn* and *reticent* are synonyms (both mean "not talkative").

Arbitrary (based on one's own will) and *tantamount* (equivalent) are not similar in meaning and therefore cannot be a pair. Therefore, the *only* possible correct answer pairs are (A) and (F), and (B) and (E). You have improved your chances from 1 in 15 to a 50/50 shot without even reading the question!

Of course, in approaching a Sentence Equivalence, you do want to analyze the sentence in the same way you would a Text Completion—read for a textual clue that tells you what type of word *must* go in the blank. Then look for a matching pair.

Strategy Tip: If you're sure that a word in the choices does *not* have a partner, cross it out! For instance, if (A) and (F) are partners and (B) and (E) are partners, and you're sure neither (C) nor (D) pair with any other answer, cross out (C) and (D) completely. They cannot be the answer together, nor can either one be part of the answer.

The sentence for the answer choice above could read as follows:

> Though the dinner guests were quite _____ , the hostess did her best to keep the conversation active and engaging.

Thus, **(B)** and **(E)** are the best choices.

Try another example:

> While athletes usually expect to achieve their greatest feats in their teens or twenties, opera singers don't reach the _____ of their vocal powers until middle age.
>
>   A   harmony
>   B   zenith
>   C   acme
>   D   terminus
>   E   nadir
>   F   cessation

<u>Solution</u>

Those with strong vocabularies might go straight to the choices to make pairs. *Zenith* and *acme* are synonyms, meaning "high point, peak." *Terminus* and *cessation* are synonyms meaning "end." *Nadir* is a low point and *harmony* is present here as a trap answer reminding you of opera singers. Cross off (A) and (E), since they do not have partners. Then, go back to the sentence, knowing that your only options are a pair meaning "peak" and a pair meaning "end."

The correct answer choices are **(B)** and **(C)**.

Math: Quantitative Comparison

In addition to regular multiple-choice questions and Data Interpretation questions, Quantitative Comparisons have been on the exam for a long time.

Each question contains a "Quantity A" and a "Quantity B," and some also contain common information that applies to both quantities. The four answer choices are always worded exactly as shown in the following example:

$$x \geq 0$$

Quantity A	**Quantity B**
x	x^2

(A) Quantity A is greater.

(B) Quantity B is greater.

(C) The two quantities are equal.

(D) The relationship cannot be determined from the information given.

<u>Solution</u>

If $x = 0$, then the two quantities are equal. If $x = 2$, then Quantity (B) is greater. Thus, you don't have enough information.

The answer is **(D)**.

Next, take a look at the new math question formats.

Math: Select One or More Answer Choices

According to the *Official Guide to the GRE revised General Test*, the official directions for "Select One or More Answer Choices" read as follows:

> <u>Directions:</u> Select one or more answer choices according to the specific question directions.
>
> If the question does not specify how many answer choices to indicate, indicate all that apply.
>
> The correct answer may be just one of the choices or as many as all of the choices, depending on the question.
>
> No credit is given unless you indicate all of the correct choices and no others.
>
> If the question specifies how many answer choices to indicate, indicate exactly that number of choices.

Note that there is <u>no partial credit</u>. If three of six choices are correct, and you indicate two of the three, no credit is given. If you are told to indicate two choices and you indicate three, no credit is given. It will also be important to read the directions carefully.

Here's a sample question:

> If $ab = |a| \times |b|$ and $ab \neq 0$, which of the following must be true?
>
> Indicate <u>all</u> such statements.
>
> A $a = b$
> B $a > 0$ and $b > 0$
> C $ab > 0$

Note that only one, only two, or all three of the choices may be correct. (Also note the word "must" in the question stem!)

1

Solution

If $ab = |a| \times |b|$, then you know ab is positive, since the right side of the equation must be positive. If ab is positive, however, that doesn't necessarily mean that a and b are each positive; it simply means that they have the same sign.

Answer choice (A) is not correct because it is not true that a must equal b; for instance, a could be 2 and b could be 3.

Answer choice (B) is not correct because it is not true that a and b must each be positive; for instance, a could be −3 and b could be −4.

Now look at choice (C). Since $|a| \times |b|$ must be positive, ab must be positive as well; that is, since two sides of an equation are, by definition, equal to one another, if one side of the equation is positive, the other side must be positive as well. Thus, answer (**C**) is correct.

Strategy Tip: Make sure to fully process the statement in the question (simplify it or list the possible scenarios) before considering the answer choices. That is, don't just look at $ab = |a| \times |b|$—rather, it's your job to draw inferences about the statement before plowing ahead. This will save you time in the long run!

Note that "indicate all that apply" didn't really make the problem harder. This is just a typical Inference-based Quant problem (for more problems like this one, see the Manhattan Prep *Number Properties* guide as well as the *Quantitative Comparisons & Data Interpretation* guide).

After all, not every real-life problem has exactly five possible solutions; why should problems on the GRE?

Math: Numeric Entry

This question type requires the test-taker to key a numeric answer into a box on the screen. You are not able to work backwards from answer choices, and in many cases, it will be difficult to make a guess. However, the principles being tested are the same as on the rest of the exam.

Here is a sample question:

If $x \triangle y = 2xy - (x - y)$, what is the value of $3 \triangle 4$?

1

Solution

You are given a function involving two variables, x and y, and asked to substitute 3 for x and 4 for y:

$$x\Delta y = 2xy - (x - y)$$
$$3\Delta 4 = 2(3)(4) - (3 - 4)$$
$$3\Delta 4 = 24 - (-1)$$
$$3\Delta 4 = 25$$

The answer is **25**.

Thus, you would type 25 into the box.

Okay. You've now got a good start on understanding the structure and question formats of the new GRE. Now it's time to begin fine-tuning your skills.

MANHATTAN
PREP

Chapter 2
of Algebra

Equations

In This Chapter...

Chapter 2

Equations

The GRE will expect you to be proficient at manipulating and solving algebraic equations. If you haven't faced equations since you were last in school, this can be intimidating. In this chapter, the objective is to help you become comfortable setting up and solving equations. You'll start with some basic equations (without the variables at first), and then work your way up to some pretty tricky problems. Time to dive in.

The Order of Operations (PEMDAS)

$$3 + 4(5-1) - 3^2 \times 2 = ?$$

Before you start dealing with variables, spend a moment looking at expressions that are made up of only numbers, such as the example above. The GRE probably won't ask you to compute something like this directly, but learning to use order of operations on numerical expressions will help you manipulate algebraic expressions and equations. So you have a string of numbers, with mathematical symbols in between them. Which part of the expression should you focus on first?

Intuitively, most people think of going in the direction they read, from left to right. When you read a book, moving left to right is a wise move (unless you're reading a language such as Chinese or Hebrew). However, when you perform basic arithmetic, there is an order that is of greater importance: **the order of operations**.

The order in which you perform the mathematical functions should primarily be determined by the functions themselves. In the correct order, the six operations are **P**arentheses, **E**xponents, **M**ultiplication/ **D**ivision, and **A**ddition/**S**ubtraction (or **PEMDAS**).

Before you solve a problem that requires PEMDAS, here's a quick review of the basic operations:

Parentheses can be written as ( ) or [ ] or even { }.

2

Exponents are $5^{2 \leftarrow \text{these numbers}}$. For example, 5^2 ("five squared") can be expressed as 5×5. In other words, it is 5 times itself two times.

Likewise, 4^3 ("four cubed," or "four to the third power") can be expressed as $4 \times 4 \times 4$ (or 4 times itself three times).

Roots are very closely related to exponents. For example, $\sqrt[3]{64}$ is the third root of 64 (commonly called the cube root). $\sqrt[3]{64}$ is basically asking the question, "What multiplied by itself three times equals 64?" This is written as $4 \times 4 \times 4 = 64$, so $\sqrt[3]{64} = 4$. The plain old square root $\sqrt{9}$ can be thought of as $\sqrt[2]{9}$. "What times itself equals 9?" The answer is $3 \times 3 = 9$, so $\sqrt{9} = 3$.

Exponents and roots can also undo each other: $\sqrt{5^2} = 5$ and $(\sqrt[3]{7^3}) = 7$.

Multiplication and **Division** can also undo each other: $2 \times 3 \div 3 = 2$ and $10 \div 5 \times 5 = 10$.

Multiplication can be expressed with parentheses: $(5)(4) = 5 \times 4 = 20$. Division can be expressed with a division sign ($\div$), a slash (/), or a fraction bar(—): $20 \div 5 = 20/5 = \dfrac{20}{5} = 4$. Also remember that multiplying or dividing by a negative number changes the sign:

$$4 \times (-2) = -8 \qquad\qquad -8 \div (-2) = 4$$

Addition and **Subtraction** can also undo each other: $8 + 7 - 7 = 8$ and $15 - 6 + 6 = 15$.

PEMDAS is a useful acronym you can use to remember the order in which operations should be performed. Some people find it useful to write PEMDAS like this:

$$\xrightarrow{\quad PE {}^{M}\!/_{D} \, {}^{A}\!/_{S} \quad}$$

For Multiplication/Division and Addition/Subtraction, perform whichever comes first from left to right. The reason that Multiplication and Division are at the same level of importance is that any Multiplication can be expressed as Division, and vice versa; for example, $7 \div 2$ is equivalent to $7 \times 1/2$. In a sense, Multiplication and Division are two sides of the same coin.

Addition and Subtraction have this same relationship: $3 - 4$ is equivalent to $3 + (-4)$. The correct order of steps to simplify this sample expression is as follows:

	$3 + 4(5 - 1) - 3^2 \times 2$
Parentheses	$3 + 4(4) - 3^2 \times 2$
Exponents	$3 + 4(4) - 9 \times 2$
Multiplication or **D**ivision (left to right)	$3 + 16 - 18$
Addition or **S**ubtraction (left to right)	$3 + 16 - 18 = 19 - 18 = 1$

Remember: If you have two operations of equal importance, you should do them in left-to-right order: $3 - 2 + 3 = 1 + 3 = 4$. The only instance in which you would override this order is when the operations are in parentheses: $3 - (2 + 3) = 3 - (5) = -2$.

Next are two problems together. Try them first on your own, then an explanation will follow:

$$5 - 3 \times 4^3 \div (7 - 1)$$

P

$5 - 3 \times 64 \div 6$

$192 \div 6 = 32$

$5 - 32 = 27$

E

$5 - 3 \times 64 \div 6 = 5 - 192 \div 6 = 5 - 32 = 27$

M/D

A/S

Your work should have looked like this:

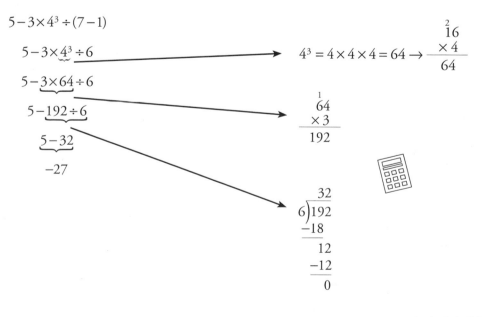

Here's one more:

$$32 \div 2^4 \times (5 - 3^2)$$

P

[handwritten: $5-9$]

[handwritten: $32 \div 2^4 \times -4$]

[handwritten: $32 \div 16 \times -4$]

E

[handwritten: $2 \times -4 = -8$]

M/D

A/S

Here's the work you should have done:

$$32 \div 2^4 \times (5 - 3^2)$$

$$32 \div 2^4 \times (5 - 9)$$

$$32 \div 2^4 \times (-4)$$

$$32 \div 16 \times (-4)$$

$$2 \times (-4)$$

$$-8$$

Check Your Skills

Evaluate the following expressions.

1. $-4 + 12/3 =$
2. $(5 - 8) \times 10 - 7 =$
3. $-3 \times 12 \div 4 \times 8 + (4 - 6) =$
4. $2^4 \times (8 \div 2 - 1)/(9 - 3) =$

Answers can be found on page 45.

MANHATTAN
PREP

Solving for a Variable with One Equation

Expressions vs. Equations

So far, you've been dealing only with expressions. Now you're going to be dealing with equations. The big difference between equations and expressions is that an equation consists of two expressions separated by an equals (or inequality) sign, while an expression lacks an equals (or inequality) sign altogether.

Pretty much everything you will be doing with equations is related to one basic principle: you can do anything you want to one side of the equation, *as long as you also do the same thing to the other side of the equation*. Take the equation $3 + 5 = 8$. You want to subtract 5 from the left side of the equation, but you still want the equation to be true. All you have to do is subtract 5 from the right side as well, and you can be confident that your new equation will still be valid:

$$\begin{array}{rcl} 3 + 5 & = & 8 \\ -5 & & -5 \\ \hline 3 & = & 3 \end{array}$$

Note that this would also work if you had variables in your equation:

$$\begin{array}{rcl} x + 5 & = & 8 \\ -5 & & -5 \\ \hline x & = & 3 \end{array}$$

Next, you're going to see some of the many ways you can apply this principle to solving algebra problems.

Solving Equations

What does it mean to solve an equation? What are you really doing when you manipulate algebraic equations?

A solution to an equation is a number that, when substituted in for the value of a variable, makes the equation *true*.

Take the equation $2x + 7 = 15$. You are looking for the value of x that will make this equation true. What if you plugged in 3 for x? If you replaced x with the number 3, you would get $2(3) + 7 = 15$. This equation can be simplified to $6 + 7 = 15$, which further simplifies to $13 = 15$. However, 13 does *not* equal 15, so when $x = 3$, the equation is *not* true. So $x = 3$ is *not* a solution to the equation.

Now, if you replaced x with the number 4, you would get $2(4) + 7 = 15$. This equation can be simplified to $8 + 7 = 15$. Simplify it further, and you get $15 = 15$, which is a true statement.

That means that when $x = 4$, the equation is true. So $x = 4$ is a solution to the equation.

Now the question becomes, what is the best way to find these solutions? If you had to use trial and error, or guessing, the process could take a very long time. The following sections will talk about how you can efficiently and accurately manipulate equations so that solutions become easier to find.

Isolating a Variable

You know that you can make a change to an equation as long as you make the same change to both sides. Now, look at the various changes you can make. Try to solve the following problem:

If $5(x-1)^3 - 30 = 10$, then $x = ?$

To solve for a variable, you need to get it by itself on one side of the equals sign. To do that, you'll need to change the appearance of the equation, but not its value. The good news is that all of the changes you will need to make to this equation to solve for x will actually be very familiar to you—PEMDAS operations!

To get x by itself, you want to move every term that *doesn't include* the variable to the other side of the equation. The easiest thing to move at this stage is the 30, so start there. If 30 is being subtracted on the left side of the equation, and you want to move it to the other side, then you need to do the opposite operation in order to cancel it out. So you're going to **add** 30 to both sides, like this:

$$
\begin{array}{rcl}
5(x-1)^3 - 30 & = & 10 \\
+30 & & +30 \\
\hline
5(x-1)^3 & = & 40
\end{array}
$$

Now you've only got one term on the left side of the equation. The x is still inside the parentheses, and the expression in the parentheses is being multiplied by 5, so the next step will be to move that 5 over to the other side of the equation. Once again, you want to perform the opposite operation, so you'll **divide** both sides of the equation by 5:

$$\frac{5(x-1)^3}{5} = \frac{40}{5} \qquad \longleftarrow \quad \text{These horizontal lines mean division.}$$

$$(x-1)^3 = 8$$

At this point, you could cube $(x-1)$, but that is going to involve a whole lot of multiplication. Instead, you can get rid of the exponent by performing the opposite operation. Roots are the opposite of exponents. So if the left side of the equation is raised to the third power, you can undo that by taking the third root of both sides, also known as the cube root, as shown below:

$$\sqrt[3]{(x-1)^3} = \sqrt[3]{8}$$

$$(x-1) = 2$$

Now that nothing else is being done to the parentheses, you can just get rid of them. The equation is:

$$x - 1 = 2$$

After that, add 1 to both sides, and you get $x = 3$. This would have been hard to guess!

Now, take a look at the steps that you took in order to isolate x. Notice anything? You *added* 30, then you *divided* by 5, then you got rid of the *exponent*, and then you simplified the *parentheses*. You did PEMDAS backwards! And, in fact, when you're isolating a variable, it turns out that the simplest way to do so is to reverse the order of PEMDAS when deciding what order you will perform your operations. Start with addition/subtraction, then multiplication/division, then exponents, and finish with terms in parentheses.

Now that you know the best way to isolate a variable, go through one more example. Try it on your own first, then an explanation will follow.

If $4\sqrt{(x-6)} + 7 = 19$, then $x = ?$

A/S

M/D

E

P

The equation you're simplifying is $4\sqrt{(x-6)} + 7 = 19$. If there's anything to add or subtract, that will be the easiest first step. There is, so the first thing you want to do is get rid of the 7 by subtracting 7 from both sides:

$$
\begin{array}{r}
4\sqrt{(x-6)} + 7 = 19 \\
\underline{-7 \quad -7} \\
4\sqrt{(x-6)} \quad = 12
\end{array}
$$

Now you want to see if there's anything being multiplied or divided by the term containing an x. The square root that contains the x is being multiplied by 4, so, your next step will be to get rid of the 4. You can do that by dividing both sides of the equation by 4:

$$\frac{\cancel{4}\sqrt{(x-6)}}{\cancel{4}} = \frac{12}{4}$$

$$\sqrt{(x-6)} = 3$$

Now that you've taken care of multiplication and division, it's time to check for exponents. And that really means you need to check for exponents and roots, because they're so intimately related. There are no exponents in the equation, but the x is inside a square root. In order to cancel out a root, you can use an exponent. Squaring a square root will cancel it out, so your next step is to square both sides:

$$\sqrt{(x-6)} = 3$$

$$\left(\sqrt{(x-6)}\right)^2 = 3^2$$

$$x - 6 = 9$$

The final step is to add 6 to both sides, and you end up with $x = 15$.

Check Your Skills

Solve for x in the following equations.

5. $3(x+4)^3 - 5 = 19$

6. $\dfrac{3x-7}{2} + 20 = 6$

7. $\sqrt[3]{(x+5)} - 7 = -8$

Answers can be found on page 45.

Equation Clean-up Moves

You've covered the basic operations that you'll be dealing with when solving equations. But what would you do if you were asked to solve for x in the following equation?

$$\frac{5x - 3(4-x)}{2x} = 10$$

Now x appears in multiple parts of the equation, and your job has become more complicated. In addition to your PEMDAS operations, you also need to be able to simplify, or clean up, your equation. There are different ways you can clean up this equation. First, notice how you have an x in the denominator (the bottom of the fraction) on the left side of the equation. You're trying to find the value of x, not of some number divided by x. So your first clean-up move is to **always get variables out of denominators**. The way to do that is to multiply both sides of the equation by the *entire* denominator. Watch what happens:

$$\cancel{2x} \times \frac{5x - 3(4 - x)}{\cancel{2x}} = 10 \times 2x$$

If you multiply a fraction by its denominator, you can cancel out the entire denominator. Now you're left with:

$$5x - 3(4 - x) = 20x$$

No more fractions! What should you do next? At some point, if you want the value of x, you're going to have to get all the terms that contain an x together. But right now, that x sitting inside the parentheses seems pretty tough to get to. To make that x more accessible, you should **simplify grouped terms within the equation**. That 3 on the outside of the parentheses wants to multiply the terms inside, so you need to **distribute** it. What that means is you're going to multiply the 3 by each and every term inside, one at a time: 3 times 4 is 12, and 3 times $-x$ is $-3x$, so the equation becomes:

$$5x - (12 - 3x) = 20x$$

Now, if you subtract what's in the parentheses from $5x$, you can get rid of the parentheses altogether. Just as you multiplied the 3 by *both* terms inside the parentheses, you also have to subtract both terms:

$$5x - (12) - (-3x) = 20x$$
$$5x - 12 + 3x = 20x$$

Remember, *subtracting a negative number is the same as adding a positive number; the negative signs cancel out!*

Now you're very close. You're ready to make use of your final clean-up move—**combine like terms**. "Like terms" are terms that can be combined into one term. For example, "$3x$" and "$5x$" are like terms because they can be combined into "$8x$." Ultimately, all the PEMDAS operations and clean-up moves have one goal—to get a variable by itself so you can determine its value. At this point, you have four terms in the equation: $5x$, -12, $3x$ and $20x$. You want to get all the terms with an x on one side of the equation, and all the terms that only contain numbers on the other side.

First, combine $5x$ and $3x$, because they're on the same side of the equation. That gives you:

$$8x - 12 = 20x$$

Now you want to get the $8x$ together with the $20x$. But which one should you move? The best move to make here is to move the $8x$ to the right side of the equation, because that way, one side of the equation will have terms that contain only numbers (-12) and the right side will have terms that contain variables ($8x$ and $20x$). So now it's time for the PEMDAS operations again. To find x:

$$8x - 12 = 20x$$
$$\underline{-8x \qquad\quad -8x}$$
$$-12 = 12x$$
$$\frac{-12}{12} = \frac{12x}{12}$$
$$-1 = x$$

2

Before moving on to the next topic, time to review what you've learned:

- **You can do whatever you want to one side of the equation, as long as you do the same thing to the other side at the same time.**

- **To isolate a variable, you should perform the PEMDAS operations in *reverse order*:**

    1. Addition/Subtraction 2. Multiplication/Division 3. Exponents/Roots 4. Parentheses

- **To clean up an equation:**

    1. Get variables out of denominators by multiplying both sides by that entire denominator.
    2. Simplify grouped terms by multiplying or distributing.
    3. Combine similar or like terms.

<u>Check Your Skills</u>

Solve for x in the following equations.

8. $\dfrac{11 + 3(x + 4)}{x - 3} = 7$

9. $\dfrac{-6 - 5(3 - x)}{2 - x} = 6$

10. $\dfrac{2x + 6(9 - 2x)}{x - 4} = -3$

Answers can be found on page 46.

Solving for Variables with Two Equations

Some GRE problems, including word problems, give you two equations, each of which has two variables. To solve such problems, you'll need to solve for one or each of those variables. At first glance, this problem may seem quite daunting:

If $3x + y = 10$ and $y = x - 2$, what is the value of y?

Maybe you've gotten pretty good at solving for one variable, but now you face two variables and two equations!

MANHATTAN
PREP

You might be tempted to test numbers, and indeed you could actually solve the above problem that way. Could you do so in under two minutes? Maybe not. Fortunately, there is a much faster way.

Substitution

One method for combining equations is called substitution. In substitution, you *insert the expression for one variable in one equation into that variable in the other equation.* The goal is to end up with one equation with one variable, because once you get a problem to that point, you know you can solve it!

There are four basic steps to substitution, which can be demonstrated with the question from above.

Step One is to isolate one of the variables in one of the equations. For this example, y is already isolated in the second equation: $y = x - 2$.

For **Step Two**, it is important to understand that the left and right sides of the equation are equivalent. This may sound obvious, but it has some interesting implications. If y equals $x - 2$, then that means you could replace the variable y with the expression $(x - 2)$ and the equation would have the same value. And, in fact, that's exactly what you're going to do. Step Two will be to go to the first equation, and substitute (hence the name) the variable y with its equivalent, $(x - 2)$. So:

$$3x + y = 10 \rightarrow 3x + (x - 2) = 10$$

Now for **Step Three**, you have one equation and one variable, so the next step is to solve for x:

$$3x + x - 2 = 10$$
$$4x = 12$$
$$x = 3$$

Now that you have a value for x, **Step Four** is to substitute that value into either original equation to solve for your second variable, y:

$$y = x - 2 \rightarrow y = (3) - 2 = 1$$

So the answer to the question is $y = 1$. **It should be noted that Step Four will only be necessary if the variable you solve for in Step Three is not the variable the question asks for.** The question asked for y, but you found x, so Step Four was needed to answer the question.

Now that you've gotten the hang of substitution, try a new problem:

If $2x + 4y = 14$ and $x - y = -8$, what is the value of x?

As you learned, the first step is to isolate your variable. Because the question asks for x, you should manipulate the second equation to isolate y. Taking this approach will make Step Four unnecessary and save you time:

2

$$x - y = -8$$
$$x = -8 + y$$
$$x + 8 = y$$

Then, for Step Two, you can substitute for y in the first equation:

$$2x + 4y = 14$$
$$2x + 4(x + 8) = 14$$

Now, for Step Three, isolate x:

$$2x + 4x + 32 = 14$$
$$6x = -18$$
$$x = -3$$

So the answer to the question is $x = -3$.

Check Your Skills

Solve for x and y in the following equations.

11. $x = 10$
     $x + 2y = 26$

12. $x + 4y = 10$
     $y - x = -5$

13. $6y + 15 = 3x$
     $x + y = 14$

Answers can be found on pages 46–47.

Subtraction of Expressions

One of the most common errors involving order of operations occurs when an expression with multiple terms is subtracted. The subtraction must occur across *every* term within the expression. Each term in the subtracted part must have its sign reversed. Here are several examples:

$x - (y - z) = x - y + z$ (Note that the signs of both y and $-z$ have been reversed.)
$x - (y + z) = x - y - z$ (Note that the signs of both y and z have been reversed.)
$x - 2(y - 3z) = x - 2y + 6z$ (Note that the signs of both y and $-3z$ have been reversed.)

What is $5x - [y - (3x - 4y)]$?

Both expressions in parentheses must be subtracted, so the signs of each term must be reversed for *each* subtraction. Note that the square brackets are just fancy parentheses, used so that you avoid having parentheses right next to each other. Work from the innermost parentheses outward:

$$5x - [y - (3x - 4y)] =$$
$$5x - [y - 3x + 4y] =$$
$$5x - y + 3x - 4y = \mathbf{8x - 5y}$$

Check Your Skills

14. Simplify: $3a - [2a - (3b - a)]$

Answer can be found on page 47.

Fraction Bars as Grouping Symbols

Even though fraction bars do not fit into the PEMDAS hierarchy, they do take precedence. In any expression with a fraction bar, you should **pretend that there are parentheses around the numerator and denominator of the fraction**. This may be obvious as long as the fraction bar remains in the expression, but it is easy to forget if you eliminate the fraction bar or add or subtract fractions, so put parentheses in to remind yourself:

$$\text{Simplify:} \frac{x-1}{2} - \frac{2x-1}{3} \rightarrow \text{Write on your paper as:} \frac{(x-1)}{2} - \frac{(2x-1)}{3}$$

The common denominator for the two fractions is 6, so multiply the numerator and denominator of the first fraction by 3, and those of the second fraction by 2:

$$\frac{(x-1)}{2}\left(\frac{3}{3}\right) - \frac{(2x-1)}{3}\left(\frac{2}{2}\right) = \frac{(3x-3)}{6} - \frac{(4x-2)}{6}$$

Once you put all numerators over the common denominator, the parentheses remind you to reverse the signs of both terms in the second numerator:

$$\frac{(3x-3)-(4x-2)}{6} = \frac{3x-3-4x+2}{6} = \frac{-x-1}{6} = -\frac{x+1}{6}$$

Check Your Skills

15. Simplify: $\dfrac{a+4}{4} - \dfrac{2a-2}{3}$

Answer can be found on page 47.

Check Your Skills Answer Key

1. **0:** $-4 + 12/3 =$ Divide first.
$-4 + 4 = 0$ Then add the two numbers.

2. **−37:** $(5 - 8) \times 10 - 7 =$
$(-3) \times 10 - 7 =$ First, combine what is inside the parentheses.
$-30 - 7 =$ Then multiply -3 and 10.
$-30 - 7 = -37$ Subtract the two numbers.

3. **−74:** $-3 \times 12 \div 4 \times 8 + (4 - 6)$
$-3 \times 12 \div 4 \times 8 + (-2)$ First, combine what's in the parentheses.
$-36 \div 4 \times 8 + (-2)$ Multiply -3 and 12.
$-9 \times 8 - 2$ Divide -36 by 4.
$-72 + (-2) = -74$ Multiply -9 by 8 and then subtract 2.

4. **8:** $2^4 \times (8 \div 2 - 1)/(9 - 3) =$
$2^4 \times (4 - 1)/(6) =$ $8/2 = 4$ and $9 - 3 = 6$.
$16 \times (3)/(6) =$ $4 - 1 = 3$ and $2^4 = 16$.
$48/6 =$ Multiply 16 by 3.
$48/6 = 8$ Divide 48 by 6.

5. **$x = -2$:** $3(x + 4)^3 - 5 = 19$
$3(x + 4)^3 - 24$ Add 5 to both sides.
$(x + 4)^3 = 8$ Divide both sides by 3.
$(x + 4) = 2$ Take the cube root of both sides.
$x = -2$ Remove the parentheses, subtract 4 from both sides.

6. **$x = -7$:** $\dfrac{3x - 7}{2} + 20 = 6$

$\dfrac{3x - 7}{2} = -14$ Subtract 20 from both sides.

$3x - 7 = -28$ Multiply both sides by 2.
$3x = -21$ Add 7 to both sides.
$x = -7$ Divide both sides by 3.

7. **$x = -6$:** $\sqrt[3]{(x + 5)} - 7 = -8$
$\sqrt[3]{(x + 5)} = -1$ Add 7 to both sides.
$x + 5 = -1$ Cube both sides, remove parentheses.
$x = -6$ Subtract 5 from both sides.

8. $x = 11$: $\dfrac{11 + 3(x + 4)}{x - 3} = 7$

$11 + 3(x + 4) = 7(x - 3)$	Multiply both sides by the denominator $(x - 3)$.
$11 + 3x + 12 = 7x - 21$	Simplify grouped terms by distributing.
$23 + 3x = 7x - 21$	Combine like terms (11 and 12.)
$23 = 4x - 21$	Subtract $3x$ from both sides.
$44 = 4x$	Add 21 to both sides.
$11 = x$	Divide both sides by 4.

9. $x = 3$: $\dfrac{-6 - 5(3 - x)}{2 - x} = 6$

$-6 - 5(3 - x) = 6(2 - x)$	Multiply both sides by the denominator $(2 - x)$.
$-6 - 15 + 5x = 12 - 6x$	Simplify grouped terms by distributing.
$-21 + 5x = 12 - 6x$	Combine like terms (-6 and -15).
$-21 + 11x = 12$	Add $6x$ to both sides.
$11x = 33$	Add 21 to both sides.
$x = 3$	Divide both sides by 11.

10. $x = 6$: $\dfrac{2x + 6(9 - 2x)}{x - 4} = -3$

$2x + 6(9 - 2x) = -3(x - 4)$	Multiply by the denominator $(x - 4)$.
$2x + 54 - 12x = -3x + 12$	Simplify grouped terms by distributing.
$-10x + 54 = -3x + 12$	Combine like terms ($2x$ and $-12x$).
$54 = 7x + 12$	Add $10x$ to both sides.
$42 = 7x$	Subtract 12 from both sides.
$6 = x$	Divide both sides by 7.

11. $x = 10, y = 8$: $\quad\quad x = 10$
$\quad\quad\quad\quad\quad\quad\quad\quad\quad x + 2y = 26$

$(10) + 2y = 26$	Substitute 10 for x in the second equation.
$2y = 16$	Subtract 10 from both sides.
$y = 8$	Divide both sides by 2.

12. $x = 6, y = 1$: $\quad\quad x + 4y = 10$
$\quad\quad\quad\quad\quad\quad\quad\quad\quad y - x = -5$

$y = x - 5$	Isolate y in the second equation.
$x + 4(x - 5) = 10$	Substitute $(x - 5)$ for y in the first equation.
$x + 4x - 20 = 10$	Simplify grouped terms within the equation.
$5x - 20 = 10$	Combine like terms (x and $4x$).
$5x = 30$	Add 20 to both sides.
$x = 6$	Divide both sides by 5.
$y - (6) = -5$	Substitute 6 for x in the second equation to solve for y.
$y = 1$	Add 6 to both sides.

MANHATTAN
PREP

13. $x = 11, y = 3$: $6y + 15 = 3x$

$\qquad\qquad\qquad\quad x + y = 14$

$2y + 5 = x$	Divide the first equation by 3.
$(2y + 5) + y = 14$	Substitute $(2y + 5)$ for x in the second equation.
$3y + 5 = 14$	Combine like terms ($2y$ and y).
$3y = 9$	Subtract 5 from both sides.
$y = 3$	Divide both sides by 3.
$x + (3) = 14$	Substitute (3) for y in the second equation to solve for x.
$x = 11$	

14. **3b:**

$3a - [2a - (3b - a)]$	Rewrite the expression carefully.
$= 3a - [2a - 3b + a]$	Distribute the minus sign and drop interior parentheses.
$= 3a - [3a - 3b]$	Combine like terms ($2a$ and a).
$= 3a - 3a + 3b$	Distribute the minus sign and drop brackets.
$= 3b$	Perform the subtraction ($3a - 3a$) to cancel those terms.

15. $\dfrac{\mathbf{20 - 5a}}{\mathbf{12}}$: $\dfrac{a + 4}{4} - \dfrac{2a - 2}{3}$

Rewrite the expression and identify the common denominator (12).

$= \dfrac{3}{3} \times \dfrac{(a + 4)}{4} - \dfrac{4}{4} \times \dfrac{(2a - 2)}{3}$

Multiply the first fraction by 3/3 and the second fraction by 4/4.

$= \dfrac{3(a + 4)}{12} - \dfrac{4(2a - 2)}{12}$

Show the products on top and bottom of each fraction.

$= \dfrac{3(a + 4) - 4(2a - 2)}{12}$

Combine the two fractions into one fraction with the common denominator.

$= \dfrac{3a + 12 - 8a + 8}{12}$

Distribute the 3 and the -4 and drop parentheses.

$= \dfrac{20 - 5a}{12}$

Combine like terms ($3a$ and $-8a$), including constraints (12 and 8).

Problem Set

1. Evaluate $-3x^2$, $-3x^3$, $3x^2$, $(-3x)^2$, and $(-3x)^3$ if $x = 2$, and also if $x = -2$

2. Evaluate $(4 + 12 \div 3 - 18) - [-11 -(-4)]$

3. Which of the parentheses in the following expressions are unnecessary and could thus be removed without any change in the value of the expression?

      (a) $-(5^2) - (12 - 7)$

      (b) $(x + y) - (w + z) - (a \times b)$

4. Evaluate $\left[\dfrac{4+8}{2-(-6)}\right] - \left[4 + 8 \div 2 - (-6)\right]$

5. Simplify: $x - (3 - x)$

6. Simplify: $(4 - y) - 2(2y - 3)$

7. Solve for x: $2(2 - 3x) - (4 + x) = 7$

8. Solve for z: $\dfrac{4z-7}{3-2z} - -5$

9.

Quantity A	**Quantity B**
$3 \times (5 + 6) \div -1$	$3 \times 5 + 6 \div -1$

10.

$$(x - 4)^3 + 11 = -16$$

Quantity A	**Quantity B**
x	-4

11.

$$2x + y = 10$$
$$3x - 2y = 1$$

Quantity A	**Quantity B**
x	y

Solutions

1.

If $x = 2$:	If $x = -2$:
$-3x^2 = -3(4) = \mathbf{-12}$	$-3x^2 = -3(4) = \mathbf{-12}$
$-3x^3 = -3(8) = \mathbf{-24}$	$-3x^3 = -3(-8) = \mathbf{24}$
$3x^2 = 3(4) = \mathbf{12}$	$3x^2 = 3(4) = \mathbf{12}$
$(-3x)^2 = (-6)^2 = \mathbf{36}$	$(-3x)^2 = 6^2 = \mathbf{36}$
$(-3x)^3 = (-6)^3 = \mathbf{-216}$	$(-3x)^3 = 6^3 = \mathbf{216}$

Remember that exponents are evaluated *before* multiplication! Watch not only the order of operations, but also the signs in these problems.

2. $\mathbf{-3}$: $(4 + 12 \div 3 - 18) - \big[-11 - (-4)\big] =$

$$(4 + 4 - 18) - (-11 + 4) =$$

$$(-10) - (-7) =$$

$$-10 + 7 = \mathbf{-3}$$

3. **(a):** The parentheses around 5^2 are unnecessary, because this exponent is performed before the negation (which counts as multiplying by -1) and before the subtraction. The other parentheses are necessary, because they cause the right-hand subtraction to be performed before the left-hand subtraction. Without them, the two subtractions would be performed from left to right.

(b): The first and last pairs of parentheses are unnecessary. The addition is performed before the neighboring subtraction by default, because addition and subtraction are performed from left to right. The multiplication is the first operation to be performed, so the right-hand parentheses are completely unnecessary. The middle parentheses are necessary to ensure that the addition is performed before the subtraction that comes to the left of it.

4. $-\dfrac{\mathbf{25}}{\mathbf{2}}$: $\left[\dfrac{4+8}{2-(-6)}\right] - \big[4 + 8 \div 2 - (-6)\big] =$

$$\left(\dfrac{4+8}{2+6}\right) - (4 + 8 \div 2 + 6) = \qquad \text{Subtraction of negative} = \text{addition.}$$

$$\left(\dfrac{12}{8}\right) - \left(4 + 4 + 6\right) = \qquad \text{Fraction bar acts as a grouping symbol.}$$

$$\dfrac{3}{2} - 14 = \qquad \text{Arithmetic}$$

$$\dfrac{3}{2} - \dfrac{28}{2} = -\dfrac{\mathbf{25}}{\mathbf{2}} \qquad \text{Arithmetic}$$

5. **$2x - 3$:** Do not forget to reverse the signs of every term in a subtracted expression:

$$x - (3 - x) = x - 3 + x = 2x - 3$$

6. **$-5y + 10$ (or $10 - 5y$):** Do not forget to reverse the signs of every term in a subtracted expression.

$$(4 - y) - 2(2y - 3) = 4 - y - 4y + 6 = -5y + 10 \text{ (or } 10 - 5y)$$

2

7. **-1:** $2(2 - 3x) - (4 + x) = 7$

$$4 - 6x - 4 - x = 7$$
$$-7x = 7$$
$$x = -1$$

8. **4/3:**

$$\frac{4z - 7}{3 - 2z} = -5$$

$$4z - 7 = -5(3 - 2z)$$
$$4z - 7 = -15 + 10z$$
$$8 = 6z$$
$$z = 8/6 = 4/3$$

9. **(B):** Evaluate Quantity A first:

$3 \times (5 + 6) \div -1$

$3 \times (11) \div -1$ Simplify the parentheses.

$33 \div -1$ Multiply and divide in order from left to right.

-33

Now evaluate Quantity B:

$3 \times 5 + 6 \div -1$

$15 + -6$ Multiply and divide in order from left to right.

9 Add.

Quantity A	**Quantity B**
-33	9

Quantity B is greater.

MANHATTAN
PREP

10. **(A):** Simplify the given equation to solve for x:

$$(x-4)^3 + 11 = -16$$

$$(x-4)^3 = -27$$

$$x - 4 = -3$$

$$x = 1$$

Quantity A	Quantity B
$x = 1$	-4

Quantity A is greater.

11. **(B):** Use substitution to solve for the values of x and y:

$2x + y = 10 \rightarrow y = 10 - 2x$	Isolate y in the first equation.
$3x - 2y = 1 \rightarrow 3x - 2(10 - 2x) = 1$	Substitute $(10 - 2x)$ for y in the second equation.
$3x - 20 + 4x = 1$	Distribute.
$7x = 21$	Group like terms ($3x$ and $4x$) and add 20 to both sides.
$x = 3$	Divide both sides by 7.
$2x + y = 10 \rightarrow 2(3) + y = 10$	Substitute 3 for x in the first equation.
$6 + y = 10$	
$y = 4$	

Quantity A	Quantity B
$x = 3$	$y = 4$

Quantity B is greater.

Chapter 3
of
Algebra

Quadratic Equations

In This Chapter...

Chapter 3
Quadratic Equations

Identifying Quadratic Equations

This section begins with a question:

> If $x^2 = 4$, what is x?

You know what to do here. Simply take the square root of both sides:

$$\sqrt{x^2} = \sqrt{4}$$
$$x = 2$$

So $x = 2$. The question seems to be answered. But, what if x were equal to -2? What would be the result? Plug -2 in for x:

$$(-2)^2 = 4 \longrightarrow 4 = 4$$

If plugging -2 in for x yields a true statement, then -2 must be a solution to the equation. But, from your initial work, you know that 2 is a solution to the equation. So which one is correct?

As it turns out, they both are. An interesting thing happens when you start raising variables to exponents. The number of possible solutions increases. When a variable is squared, as in the example above, it becomes possible that there will be two solutions to the equation.

What this means is that whenever you see an equation with a squared variable, you need to:

- Recognize that the equation may have two solutions.
- Know how to find both solutions.

A quadratic equation is any equation for which the highest power on a variable is the second power (e.g., x^2).

For an equation such as $x^2 = 25$ or $x^2 = 9$, finding both solutions shouldn't be too challenging. Take a minute to find both solutions for each equation.

You should have found that x equals either 5 or -5 in the first equation, and 3 or -3 in the second equation. But what if you are asked to solve for x in the following equation?

$$x^2 + 3x - 10 = 0$$

Unfortunately, you don't yet have the ability to deal with equations like this, which is why the next part of this chapter will deal with some more important tools for manipulating and solving **quadratic equations: distributing and factoring**.

Distributing

You first came across distributing when you were learning how to clean up equations and isolate a variable. Essentially, distributing is applying multiplication across a sum.

To review, if you are presented with the expression $3(x + 2)$, and you want to simplify it, you have to distribute the 3 so that it is multiplied by both the x and the 2:

$$3(x + 2) \rightarrow (3 \times x) + (3 \times 2) \rightarrow 3x + 6$$

But what if the first part of the multiplication is more complicated? Suppose you need to simplify $(a + b)(x + y)$?

Simplifying this expression is really an extension of the principle of distribution—every term in the first part of the expression must multiply every term in the second part of the expression. In order to do so correctly every time, you can use a handy acronym to remember the steps necessary: FOIL. The letters stand for **F**irst, **O**uter, **I**nner, **L**ast.

In this case, it looks like this:

$(\boldsymbol{a} + b)(\boldsymbol{x} + y)$ F – multiply the first term in each of the parentheses: $a \times x = ax$.
$(\boldsymbol{a} + b)(x + \boldsymbol{y})$ O – multiply the outer term in each: $a \times y = ay$.
$(a + \boldsymbol{b})(\boldsymbol{x} + y)$ I – multiply the inner term in each: $b \times x = bx$.
$(a + \boldsymbol{b})(x + \boldsymbol{y})$ L – multiply the last term in each: $b \times y = by$.

So you have $(a + b)(x + y) = ax + ay + bx + by$.

You can verify this system with numbers. Take the expression $(3 + 4)(10 + 20)$. This is no different than multiplying $(7)(30)$, which gives you 210. See what happens when you FOIL the numbers:

$(\boldsymbol{3} + 4)(\boldsymbol{10} + 20)$ F – multiply the first term in each of the parentheses: $3 \times 10 = 30$.
$(\boldsymbol{3} + 4)(10 + \boldsymbol{20})$ O – multiply the outer term in each: $3 \times 20 = 60$.
$(3 + \boldsymbol{4})(\boldsymbol{10} + 20)$ I – multiply the inner term in each: $4 \times 10 = 40$.
$(3 + \boldsymbol{4})(10 + \boldsymbol{20})$ L – multiply the last term in each: $4 \times 20 = 80$.

Finally, sum the four products: $30 + 60 + 40 + 80 = 210$.

Now that you have the basics down, go through a more GRE-like situation. Take the expression $(x + 2)$ $(x + 3)$. Once again, begin by FOILing it:

$(\boldsymbol{x} + 2)(\boldsymbol{x} + 3)$	F – multiply the first term in each of the parentheses: $x \times x = x^2$.
$(\boldsymbol{x} + 2)(x + \boldsymbol{3})$	O – multiply the outer term in each: $x \times 3 = 3x$.
$(x + \boldsymbol{2})(\boldsymbol{x} + 3)$	I – multiply the inner term in each: $2 \times x = 2x$.
$(x + \boldsymbol{2})(x + \boldsymbol{3})$	L – multiply the last term in each: $2 \times 3 = 6$.

The expression becomes $x^2 + 3x + 2x + 6$. Combine like terms, and you are left with $x^2 + 5x + 6$. The next section will discuss the connection between distributing, factoring, and solving quadratic equations. But for the moment, practice FOILing expressions.

Check Your Skills

FOIL the following expressions.

1. $(x + 4)(x + 9)$
2. $(y + 3)(y - 6)$
3. $(x + 7)(3 + x)$

Answers can be found on page 71.

Factoring

What is factoring? *Factoring is the process of reversing the distribution of terms.*

For example, when you multiply y and $(5 - y)$, you get $5y - y^2$. Reversing this, if you're given $5y - y^2$, you can "factor out" a y to transform the expression into $y(5 - y)$. Another way of thinking about factoring is that you're *pulling out* a common term and rewriting the expression as a *product*.

You can factor out many different things on the GRE: variables, variables with exponents, numbers, and expressions with more than one term, such as $(y - 2)$ or $(x + w)$. Here are some examples:

$t^2 + t$ $= t(t + 1)$	Factor out a t. Notice that a 1 remains behind when you factor a t out of a t.
$5k^3 - 15k^2$ $= 5k^2(k - 3)$	Factor out a $5k^2$.
$21j + 35k$ $= 7(3j + 5k)$	Factor out a 7; since the variables are different, you can't factor out any variables.

If you ever doubt whether you've factored correctly, just distribute back. For instance, $t(t + 1) = t \times t + t \times 1 = t^2 + t$, so $t(t + 1)$ is the correct factored form of $t^2 + t$.

You should factor expressions for several reasons. One common reason is to simplify an expression (the GRE complicates equations that are actually quite simple). The other reason, which will be discussed in more detail shortly, is to find possible values for a variable or combination of variables.

Check Your Skills

Factor the following expressions.

4. $4 + 8t$
5. $5x + 25y$
6. $2x^2 + 16x^3$

Answers can be found on page 71.

How Do You Apply This to Quadratics?

If you were told that $7x = 0$, you would know that x must be 0. This is because the only way to make the product of two or more numbers equal 0 is to have at least one of those numbers equal 0. Clearly, 7 does not equal 0, which means that x must be 0.

Now, what if you were told that $kj = 0$? Well, now you have two possibilities. If $k = 0$, then $0(j) = 0$, which is true, so $k = 0$ is a solution to the equation $kj = 0$. Likewise, if $j = 0$, then $k(0) = 0$, which is also true, so $j = 0$ is also a solution to $kj = 0$.

Either of these scenarios make the equation true, and in fact are the only scenarios that make the product $kj = 0$. (If this is not clear, try plugging in non-zero numbers for both k and j and see what happens.)

So this is why you want to rewrite quadratic equations such as $x^2 + 3x - 10 = 0$ in factored form: $(x + 5)(x - 2) = 0$. The left side of the factored equation is a *product*, so it's really the same thing as $jk = 0$. Now you know that either $x + 5$ is 0, or $x - 2$ is 0. This means either $x = -5$ or $x = 2$. Once you've factored a quadratic equation, it's straightforward to find the solutions.

Check Your Skills

List all possible solutions to the following equations.

7. $(x - 2)(x - 1) = 0$
8. $(x + 4)(x + 5) = 0$
9. $(y - 3)(y + 6) = 0$

Answers can be found on page 71.

Factoring Quadratic Equations

Okay, so now you understand *why* you want to factor a quadratic expression, but *how* do you do it? It's not easy to look at $x^2 + 3x - 10$ and see that it equals $(x + 5)(x - 2)$.

To get started, try solving the puzzle below. (Hint: It involves addition and multiplication.) The first two are done for you:

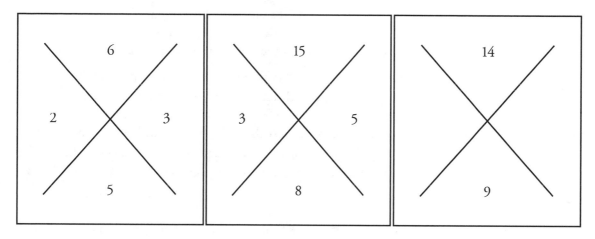

Have you figured out the trick to this puzzle? The answers are below.

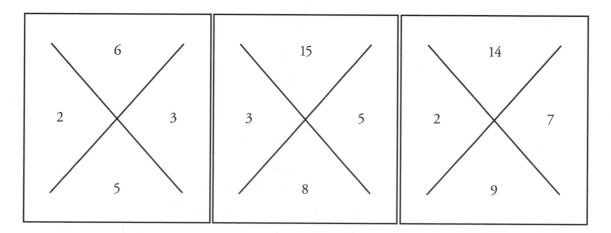

The way the diamonds work is that you multiply the two numbers on the sides to obtain the top number, and you add them to arrive at the bottom number.

Take another look at the connection between $(x + 2)(x + 3)$ and $x^2 + 5x + 6$:

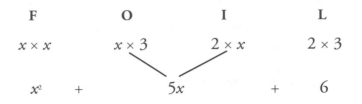

The 2 and the 3 play two important roles in building the quadratic expression:

- They multiply together to give you 6, which is the final term in your quadratic expression.

- Multiplying the outer terms gives you $3x$, and multiplying the inner terms gives you $2x$. You can then add those terms to get $5x$, the middle term of your quadratic expression.

So when you are trying to factor a quadratic expression such as $x^2 + 5x + 6$, the key is to find the two numbers whose product equals the final term (6) and whose sum equals the coefficient of the middle term (the 5 in $5x$). In this case, the two numbers that multiply to 6 and add up to 5 are 2 and 3: $2 \times 3 = 6$ and $2 + 3 = 5$.

So the diamond puzzle is just a visual representation of this same goal. For any quadratic expression, take the final term (the **constant**) and place it in the top portion of the diamond. Take the **coefficient** of the middle term (in this case, the "5" in "$5x$") and place it in the lower portion of the diamond. For instance, if the middle term is $5x$, take the 5 and place it at the bottom of the diamond. Now go through the entire process with a new example: $x^2 + 7x + 12$.

The final term is 12, and the coefficient of the middle term is 7, so the diamond will look like this:

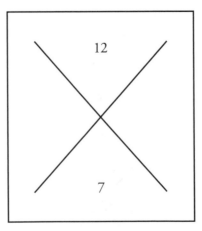

When factoring quadratics (or solving the diamond puzzle), it is better to focus first on determining which numbers could multiply to the final term. The reason is that these problems typically deal only with integers, and there are far fewer pairs of integers that will multiply to a certain product than will add to a certain sum. For instance, in this problem, there are literally an infinite number of integer pairs that can add to 7 (remember, negative numbers are also integers: $-900,000$ and $900,007$ sum to 7, for instance). On the other hand, there are only a few integer pairs that multiply to 12. You can actually

MANHATTAN
PREP

list them all out: 1 and 12, 2 and 6, and 3 and 4. Because 1 and 12 sum to 13, they don't work; 2 and 6 sum to 8, so they don't work either. However, 3 and 4 sum to 7, so this pair of numbers is the one you want. So your completed diamond looks like this:

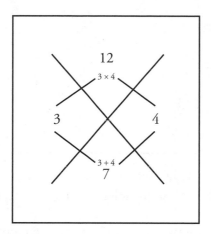

Now, because your numbers are **3** and **4**, the factored form of your quadratic expression becomes $(x + 3)(x + 4)$.

Note: if you are factoring $x^2 + 7x + 12 = 0$, you get $(x + 3)(x + 4) = 0$, so your solutions are *negative* 3 or *negative* 4, not 3 and 4 themselves. Remember, if you have $(x + 3)(x + 4) = 0$, then either $x + 3 = 0$ or $x + 4 = 0$.

Here's try another example with one important difference. Solve the diamond puzzle for this quadratic expression: $x^2 - 9x + 18$. Your diamond looks like this:

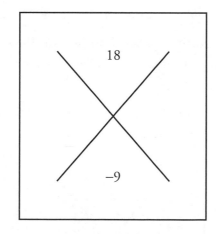

Now you need two numbers that multiply to positive 18, but sum to −9. Here, you know the product is positive, but the sum is negative. So when the top number is positive and the bottom number is negative, the two numbers you are looking for will both be negative.

Once again, it will be easier to start by figuring out what pairs of numbers can multiply to 18. In this case, three different pairs all multiply to 18: −1 and −18, −2 and −9, and −3 and −6. The pair −3 and −6, however, is the only pair of numbers that also sums to −9, so this is the pair you want. Fill in the missing numbers, and your diamond becomes:

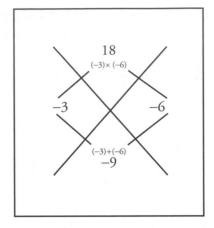

Now, if the numbers on the left and right of the diamond are **−3** and **−6**, the factored form of the quadratic expression becomes $(x - 3)(x - 6)$, so the solutions are *positive* 3 or *positive* 6.

To recap, when the final term of the quadratic is positive, the two numbers you are looking for will either both be positive or both be negative. If the middle term is positive, as in the case of $x^2 + 7x + 12$, the numbers will both be positive (3 and 4). If the middle term is negative, as in the case of $x^2 - 9x + 18$, the numbers will both be negative (−3 and −6).

Check Your Skills

Factor the following quadratic expressions.

10. $x^2 + 14x + 33$
11. $x^2 - 14x + 45$

Answers can be found on page 72.

The previous section dealt with quadratic equations in which the final term was positive. This section discusses how to deal with quadratics in which the final term is negative. The basic method is the same, although there is one important twist.

Take a look at the quadratic expression $x^2 + 3x - 10$. Start by creating your diamond:

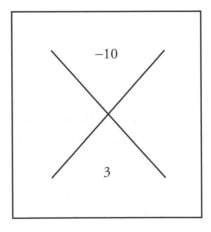

You are looking for two numbers that will multiply to −10. The only way for the product of two numbers to be negative is for one of them to be positive and one of them to be negative. That means that

in addition to figuring out pairs of numbers that multiply to 10, you also need to worry about which number will be positive and which will be negative. Disregard the signs for the moment. There are only two pairs of integers that multiply to 10: 1 and 10 and 2 and 5. Start testing out the pair 1 and 10, and see what you can learn.

Try making 1 positive and 10 negative. If that were the case, the factored form of the expression would be $(x + 1)(x - 10)$. FOIL it out and see what it would look like:

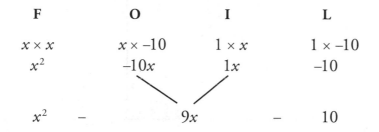

The sum of 1 and -10 is -9, but you want 3. That's not correct, so try reversing the signs. Now see what happens if you make 1 negative and 10 positive. The factored form would now be $(x - 1)(x + 10)$. Once again, FOIL it out:

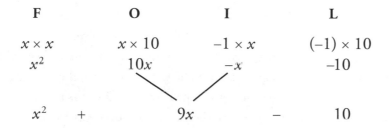

Again, this doesn't match your target. The sum of -1 and 10 is not 3. Compare these examples to the examples in the last section. Notice that, with the examples in the last section, the two numbers summed to the coefficient of the middle term (in the example $x^2 + 7x + 12$, the two numbers you wanted, 3 and 4, summed to 7, which is the coefficient of the middle term). In these two examples, however, because one number was positive and one number was negative, it is actually the *difference* of 1 and 10 that gave us the coefficient of the middle term.

This will be discussed further as the example continues. For now, to factor quadratics in which the final term is negative, you actually ignore the sign initially and look for two numbers that multiply to the coefficient of the final term (ignoring the sign) and whose *difference* is the coefficient of the middle term (ignoring the sign).

Back to the example. The pair of numbers 1 and 10 did not work, so look at the pair 2 and 5. Notice that the coefficient of the middle term is 3, and the difference of 2 and 5 is 3. This has to be the correct pair, so all you need to do is determine whether your factored form is $(x + 2)(x - 5)$ *or* $(x - 2)(x + 5)$. Take some time now to FOIL both expressions and figure out which one is correct. The correct answer is on the next page.

You should have come to the conclusion that $(x-2)(x+5)$ was the correctly factored form of the expression. That means your diamond looks like this:

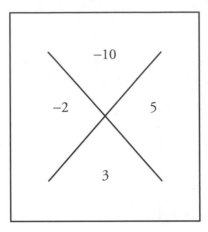

To recap, the way to factor *any* quadratic expression where the final term is negative is as follows:

1. Ignore the signs initially. Find a pair of numbers that multiply to the coefficient of the final term and whose *difference* is the coefficient of the middle term (for $x^2 + 3x - 10$, the numbers 2 and 5 multiply to 10 and $5 - 2 = 3$).

2. Now that you have the pair of numbers (2 and 5), you need to figure out which one will be positive and which one will be negative. As it turns out, this is straightforward to do. Pay attention to signs again. If the sign of the middle term is positive, then the greater of the two numbers will be positive, and the smaller will be negative. This was the case in the previous example. The middle term was +3, so the pair of numbers was +5 and −2. On the other hand, when the middle term is negative, the greater number will be negative, and the smaller number will be positive.

Work through one more example to see how this works. What is the factored form of $x^2 - 4x - 21$? Take some time to work through it for yourself, and then see the explanation on the next page.

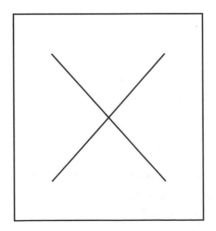

First, start your diamond. It looks like this:

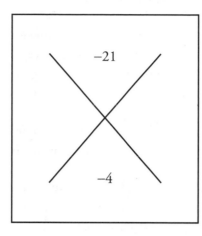

Because the coefficient of the final term (−21) is negative, you're going to ignore the signs for the moment, and focus on finding pairs of integers that will multiply to 21. The only possible pairs are 1 and 21, and 3 and 7. Next, take the difference of both pairs: 21 − 1 = 20 and 7 − 3 = 4. The second pair matches the −4 on the bottom of the diamond (because you are ignoring the sign of the −4 at this stage), so 3 and 7 is the correct pair of numbers.

Now all that remains is to determine the sign of each. The coefficient of the middle term (−4) is negative, so you need to assign the negative sign to the greater of the two numbers, 7. That means that the 3 will be positive. So the correctly factored form of the quadratic expression is $(x + 3)(x − 7)$:

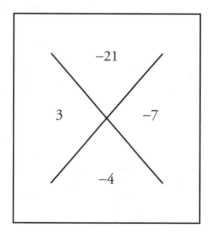

Check Your Skills

Factor the following expressions.

12. $x^2 + 3x − 18$
13. $x^2 − 5x − 66$

Answers can be found on pages 72–73.

Solving Quadratic Equations

Now that you know how to factor quadratic expressions, it's time to make that final jump to actually solving quadratic equations. When first discussing factoring, it was noted that when one side of the equation is equal to 0, you can make use of the rule that anything times 0 is 0. In the case of the equation $(x - 5)(x + 10) = 0$, you know that either $(x - 5) = 0$ or $(x + 10) = 0$, which means that $x = 5$ *or* $x = -10$.

The whole point of factoring quadratic equations is so that you can make use of this rule. That means that, before you factor a quadratic expression, you *must* make sure that the other side of the equation equals 0.

Suppose you see an equation $x^2 + 10x = -21$, and you need to solve for x. The x^2 term in the equation should tell you that this is a quadratic equation, but it's not yet ready to be factored. Before it can be factored, you have to move everything to one side of the equation. In this equation, the easiest way to do that is to add 21 to both sides, giving you $x^2 + 10x + 21 = 0$. Now that one side equals 0, you are ready to factor.

The final term is positive, so you're looking for two numbers to multiply to 21 and sum to 10. The numbers 3 and 7 fit the bill, so your factored form is $(x + 3)(x + 7) = 0$. That means that $x = -3$ *or* $x = -7$.

And now you know all the steps to successfully factoring and solving quadratic equations.

Check Your Skills

Solve the following quadratic equations.

14. $x^2 - 3x + 2 = 0$
15. $x^2 + 2x - 35 = 0$
16. $x^2 - 15x = -26$

Answers can be found on pages 73–74.

Using FOIL with Square Roots

Some GRE problems ask you to solve factored expressions that involve roots. For example, the GRE might ask you to solve the following:

What is the value of $(\sqrt{8} - \sqrt{3})(\sqrt{8} + \sqrt{3})$?

Even though these problems do not involve any variables, you can solve them just like you would solve a pair of quadratic factors: use FOIL:

First:	$\sqrt{8} \times \sqrt{8} = 8$		**Outer:**	$\sqrt{8} \times \sqrt{3} = \sqrt{24}$
Inner:	$\sqrt{8} \times \left(-\sqrt{3}\right) = -\sqrt{24}$		**Last:**	$\left(-\sqrt{3}\right)\left(\sqrt{3}\right) = -3$

The four terms are: $8 + \sqrt{24} - \sqrt{24} - 3$.

You can simplify this expression by removing the two middle terms (they cancel each other out) and subtracting: $8 + \sqrt{24} - \sqrt{24} - 3 = 8 - 3 = 5$. Although the problem looks complex, using FOIL reduces the entire expression to 5.

Check Your Skills

17. FOIL $(\sqrt{8} - \sqrt{2})(\sqrt{8} - \sqrt{2})$

Answer can be found on page 74.

One-Solution Quadratics

Not all quadratic equations have two solutions. Some have only one solution. One-solution quadratics are also called **perfect square** quadratics, because both roots are the same. Consider the following examples:

$$x^2 + 8x + 16 = 0$$
$$(x + 4)(x + 4) = 0$$
$$(x + 4)^2 = 0$$

Here, the one solution for x is -4.

$$x^2 - 6x + 9 = 0$$
$$(x - 3)(x - 3) = 0$$
$$(x - 3)^2 = 0$$

Here, the one solution for x is 3.

Be careful not to assume that a quadratic equation always has two solutions. Always factor quadratic equations to determine their solutions. In doing so, you will see whether a quadratic equation has one or two solutions.

Check Your Skills

18. Solve for x: $x^2 - 10x + 25 = 0$

Answer can be found on page 74.

Zero in the Denominator: Undefined

Math convention does not allow division by 0. When 0 appears in the denominator of an expression, then that expression is undefined. How does this convention affect quadratic equations? Consider the following:

What are the solutions to the following equation?

$$\frac{x^2 + x - 12}{x - 2} = 0$$

Notice a quadratic equation in the numerator. Since it is a good idea to start solving quadratic equations by factoring, factor this numerator as follows:

$$\frac{x^2 + x - 12}{x - 2} = 0 \rightarrow \frac{(x-3)(x+4)}{x-2} = 0$$

If either of the factors in the numerator is 0, then the entire expression becomes 0. Thus, the solutions to this equation are $x = 3$ or $x = -4$.

Note that making the denominator of the fraction equal to 0 would *not* make the entire expression equal to 0. Recall that if 0 appears in the denominator, the expression becomes undefined. Thus, $x = 2$ (which would make the denominator equal to 0) is *not* a solution to this equation. In fact, since setting x equal to 2 would make the denominator 0, the value 2 is not allowed: **x cannot equal 2**.

Check Your Skills

19. Solve for x: $\dfrac{(x+1)(x-2)}{(x-4)} = 0$

Answer can be found on page 74.

The Three Special Products

Three quadratic expressions called *special products* come up so frequently on the GRE that it pays to memorize them. You should immediately recognize these three expressions and know how to factor (or distribute) each one automatically. This will usually put you on the path toward the solution to the problem:

Special Product #1: $x^2 - y^2 = (x + y)(x - y)$

Special Product #2: $x^2 + 2xy + y^2 = (x + y)(x + y) = (x + y)^2$

Special Product #3: $x^2 - 2xy + y^2 = (x - y)(x - y) = (x - y)^2$

You should be able to identify these products when they are presented in disguised form. For example, $a^2 - 1$ can be factored as $(a + 1)(a - 1)$. Similarly, $(a + 1)^2$ can be distributed as $a^2 + 2a + 1$.

Avoid the following common mistakes with special products:

Wrong: $(x + y)^2 = x^2 + y^2$?   Right: $(x + y)^2 = x^2 + 2xy + y^2$
$(x - y)^2 = x^2 - y^2$? $(x - y)^2 = x^2 - 2xy + y^2$

Check Your Skills

Factor the following.

20. $4a^2 + 4ab + b^2 = 0$
21. $x^2 + 22xy + 121y^2 = 0$

Answers can be found on page 74.

MANHATTAN
PREP

Check Your Skills Answer Key

1. $x^2 + 13x + 36$: $(x + 4)(x + 9)$

$(\boldsymbol{x} + 4)(\boldsymbol{x} + 9)$	F – multiply the first term in each parentheses: $x \times x = x^2$.
$(\boldsymbol{x} + 4)(x + \boldsymbol{9})$	O – multiply the outer term in each: $x \times 9 = 9x$.
$(x + \boldsymbol{4})(\boldsymbol{x} + 9)$	I – multiply the inner term in each: $4 \times x = 4x$.
$(x + \boldsymbol{4})(x + \boldsymbol{9})$	L – multiply the last term in each: $4 \times 9 = 36$.

$x^2 + 9x + 4x + 36 \rightarrow x^2 + 13x + 36$

2. $y^2 - 3y - 18$: $(y + 3)(y - 6)$

$(\boldsymbol{y} + 3)(\boldsymbol{y} - 6)$	F – multiply the first term in each parentheses: $y \times y = y^2$.
$(\boldsymbol{y} + 3)(y - \boldsymbol{6})$	O – multiply the outer term in each: $y \times -6 = -6y$.
$(y + \boldsymbol{3})(\boldsymbol{y} - 6)$	I – multiply the inner term in each: $3 \times y = 3y$.
$(y + \boldsymbol{3})(y - \boldsymbol{6})$	L – multiply the last term in each: $3 \times -6 = -18$.

$y^2 - 6y + 3y - 18 \rightarrow y^2 - 3y - 18$

3. $x^2 + 10x + 21$: $(x + 7)(3 + x)$

$(\boldsymbol{x} + 7)(\boldsymbol{3} + x)$	F – multiply the first term in each parentheses: $x \times 3 = 3x$.
$(\boldsymbol{x} + 7)(3 + \boldsymbol{x})$	O – multiply the outer term in each: $x \times x = x^2$.
$(x + \boldsymbol{7})(\boldsymbol{3} + x)$	I – multiply the inner term in each: $7 \times 3 = 21$.
$(x + \boldsymbol{7})(3 + \boldsymbol{x})$	L – multiply the last term in each: $7 \times x = 7x$.

$3x + x^2 + 21 + 7x \rightarrow x^2 + 10x + 21$

4. $4 + 8t$

$\boldsymbol{4(1 + 2t)}$ Factor out a 4.

5. $5x + 25y$

$\boldsymbol{5(x + 5y)}$ Factor out a 5.

6. $2x^2 + 16x^3$

$\boldsymbol{2x^2(1 + 8x)}$ Factor out a $2x^2$.

7. $x = 2$ OR 1: $(x - 2)(x - 1) = 0$

$(x - 2) = 0 \rightarrow x = 2$	Remove the parentheses and solve for x.
OR $(x - 1) = 0 \rightarrow x = 1$	Remove the parentheses and solve for x.

8. $x = -4$ OR -5: $(x + 4)(x + 5) = 0$

$(x + 4) = 0 \rightarrow x = -4$	Remove the parentheses and solve for x.
OR $(x + 5) = 0 \rightarrow x = -5$	Remove the parentheses and solve for x.

9. $y = 3$ OR -6: $(y - 3)(y + 6) = 0$

$(y - 3) = 0 \rightarrow y = 3$	Remove the parentheses and solve for y.
OR $(y + 6) = 0 \rightarrow y = -6$	Remove the parentheses and solve for y.

10. **(x + 3)(x + 11):** $x^2 + 14x + 33$

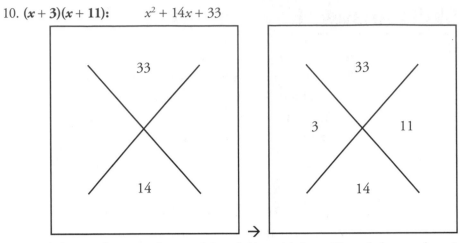

The numbers 1 and 33 and 3 and 11 multiply to 33, and the numbers 3 and 11 sum to 14
$(x + 3)(x + 11)$

11. **(x − 5)(x − 9):** $x^2 − 14x + 45$

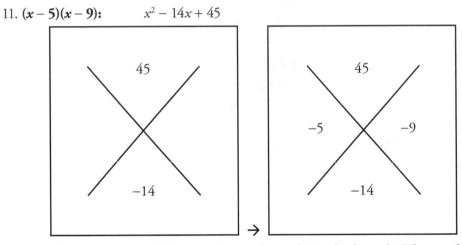

The numbers 1 and 45, 3 and 15, and 5 and 9 multiply to 45. The numbers 5 and 9 sum to 14.
$(x − 5)(x − 9)$

12. **(x + 6)(x − 3):** $x^2 + 3x − 18$

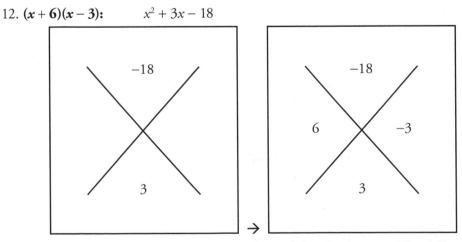

The numbers 1 and 18, 2 and 9, and 3 and 6 multiply to 18. The difference of 3 and 6 is 3.
The middle term is positive, so the greater of the two numbers (6) is positive.
$(x + 6)(x − 3)$

13. **$(x + 6)(x - 11)$:** $x^2 - 5x - 66$

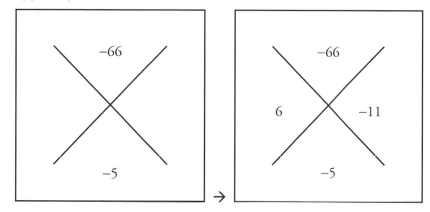

The numbers 1 and 66, 2 and 33, 3 and 22, and 6 and 11 multiply to 66.
The difference of 6 and 11 is 5.
$(x + 6)(x - 11)$

14. **$x = 1$ OR 2:** $x^2 - 3x + 2 = 0$

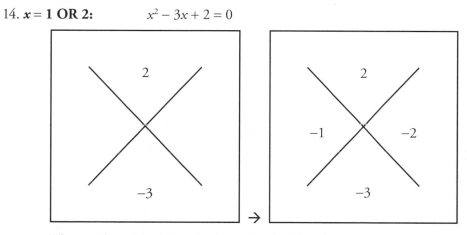

The numbers 1 and 2 multiply to 2 and add to 3.
$(x - 1)(x - 2) = 0$

15. **$x = 5$ OR -7:** $x^2 + 2x - 35 = 0$

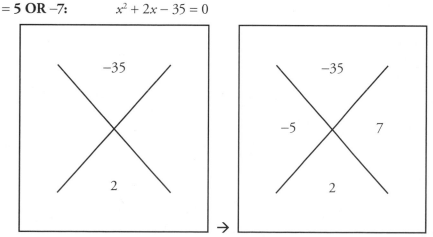

The numbers 5 and 7 multiply to 35 and their difference is 2. The middle term is positive, so
the greater of the two numbers (7) is positive. Thus, $(x - 5)(x + 7) = 0$

16. **$x = 2$ OR 13:** $x^2 - 15x = -26$

$x^2 - 15x + 26 = 0$ Add 26 to both sides so that the expression equals 0.

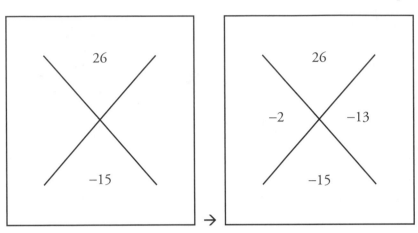

The numbers 2 and 13 multiply to 26 and sum to 15.

$(x - 2)(x - 13) = 0$

17. **2:** FOIL $(\sqrt{8} - \sqrt{2})(\sqrt{8} - \sqrt{2})$

First: $\sqrt{8} \times \sqrt{8} = 8$

Outer: $\sqrt{8} \times (-\sqrt{2}) = -\sqrt{16} = -4$

Inner: $(-\sqrt{2}) \times \sqrt{8} = -\sqrt{16} = -4$

Last: $\sqrt{2} \times \sqrt{2} = 2$

Sum of FOIL terms: $8 - 4 - 4 + 2 = 2$

18. **$x = 5$:** $x^2 - 10x + 25 = 0$

$(x - 5)(x - 5) = 0$

$x = 5$

19. **$x = -1, 2; x \neq 4$:** $\dfrac{(x+1)(x-2)}{(x-4)} = 0$

The numerator is 0 if either $(x + 1)$ or $(x - 2)$ is 0. Thus, $x = -1$ or $x = 2$. But $x \neq 4$, because $x = 4$ would make the fraction undefined.

20. **$(2a + b)^2 = 0$:** $4a^2 + 4ab + b^2 = 0 \rightarrow (2a)^2 + 2(2a)(b) + b^2 = 0 \rightarrow (2a + b)(2a + b) = 0$

21. **$(x + 11y)^2 = 0$:** $x^2 + 22xy + 121y^2 = 0 \rightarrow x^2 + 2x(11y) + (11y)^2 = 0 \rightarrow (x + 11y)(x + 11y) = 0$

MANHATTAN
PREP

Problem Set

Solve the following problems. Distribute and factor when needed.

1. If -4 is a solution for x in the equation $x^2 + kx + 8 = 0$, what is k?

2. If 8 and -4 are the solutions for x, which of the following could be the equation?

    (A) $x^2 - 4x - 32 = 0$ (B) $x^2 - 4x + 32 = 0$ (C) $x^2 + 4x - 12 = 0$
    (D) $x^2 + 4x + 32 - 0$ (E) $x^2 + 4x + 12 = 0$

3. If $16 - y^2 = 10(4 + y)$, what is y?

4. If $x^2 - 10 = -1$, what is x?

5. If $x^2 - 13x = 30$, what is x?

6. If the area of a certain square (expressed in square meters) is added to its perimeter (expressed in meters), the sum is 77. What is the length of a side of the square?

7. Hugo lies on top of a building, throwing pennies straight down to the street below. The formula for the height in meters, H, that a penny falls is $H = Vt + 5t^2$, where V is the original velocity of the penny (how fast Hugo throws it as it leaves his hand in meters per second) and t is equal to the time it takes to hit the ground in seconds. The building is 60 meters high, and Hugo throws the penny down at an initial speed of 20 meters per second. How long does it take for the penny to hit the ground?

8. $(3 - \sqrt{7})(3 + \sqrt{7}) = ?$

9. If $x^2 - 6x - 27 = 0$ and $y^2 - 6y - 40 = 0$, what is the maximum value of $x + y$?

10. If $x^2 - 10x + 25 = 16$, what is x?

11. $x^2 - 2x - 15 = 0$

Quantity A	**Quantity B**
x	1

12. $x^2 - 12x + 36 = 0$

Quantity A	**Quantity B**
x	6

13. $xy > 0$

Quantity A	**Quantity B**
$(x + y)^2$	$(x - y)^2$

Solutions

1. $k = 6$: If -4 is a solution, then you know that $(x + 4)$ must be one of the factors of the quadratic equation. The other factor is $(x + ?)$. You know that the product of 4 and ? must be equal to 8; thus, the other factor is $(x + 2)$. You know that the sum of 4 and 2 must be equal to k. Therefore, $k = 6$.

2. **(A):** If the solutions to the equation are 8 and -4, the factored form of the equation is:

$$(x - 8)(x + 4) = 0$$

Distributed, this equals: $x^2 - 4x - 32 = 0$.

3. $y = \{-4, -6\}$: Simplify and factor to solve.

$$16 - y^2 = 10(4 + y)$$
$$16 - y^2 = 40 + 10y$$
$$y^2 + 10y + 24 = 0$$
$$(y + 4)(y + 6) = 0$$

$$y + 4 = 0 \qquad or \qquad y + 6 = 0$$
$$y = -4 \qquad\qquad\qquad y = -6$$

Notice that it is possible to factor the left-hand side of the equation first: $16 - y^2 = (4 + y)(4 - y)$. However, doing so is potentially dangerous: you may decide to then divide both sides of the equation by $(4 + y)$. You cannot do this, because it is possible that $(4 + y)$ equals 0 (and, in fact, for one solution of the equation, it does!).

4. $x = \{-3, 3\}$:

Alternatively:

$$x^2 - 10 = -1 \qquad\qquad\qquad x^2 - 9 = 0$$
$$x^2 = 9 \qquad\qquad\qquad (x - 3)(x + 3) = 0$$
$$x = \{-3, 3\} \qquad\qquad\qquad x = \{3, -3\}$$

5. $x = \{15, -2\}$:

$$x^2 - 13x = 30$$
$$x^2 - 13x - 30 = 0$$
$$(x + 2)(x - 15) = 0$$

$$x + 2 = 0 \qquad or \qquad x - 15 = 0$$
$$x = -2 \qquad or \qquad x = 15$$

6. $s = 7$: The area of the square $= s^2$. The perimeter of the square $= 4s$:

$$s^2 + 4s = 77$$
$$s^2 + 4s - 77 = 0$$
$$(s + 11)(s - 7) = 0$$

$$s + 11 = 0 \qquad\qquad s - 7 = 0$$
$$s = -11 \qquad or \qquad s = 7$$

Since the edge of a square must be positive, discard the negative value for s.

7. **$t = 2$:**

$$H = Vt + 5t^2$$
$$60 = 20t + 5t^2$$
$$5t^2 + 20t - 60 = 0$$
$$5(t^2 + 4t - 12) = 0$$
$$5(t + 6)(t - 2) = 0$$

$t + 6 = 0$		$t - 2 = 0$
$t = -6$	*or*	$t = 2$

Since a time must be positive, discard the negative value for t.

8. **2:** Use FOIL to simplify this product:

F: $3 \times 3 = 9$

O: $3 \times \sqrt{7} = 3\sqrt{7}$

I: $-\sqrt{7} \times 3 = -3\sqrt{7}$

L: $-\sqrt{7} \times \sqrt{7} = -7$

$9 + 3\sqrt{7} - 3\sqrt{7} - 7 = 2$

9. **19:** Factor both quadratic equations. Then use the greatest possible values of x and y to find the maximum value of the sum $x + y$:

$$x^2 - 6x - 27 = 0 \qquad\qquad y^2 - 6y - 40 = 0$$
$$(x + 3)(x - 9) = 0 \qquad\qquad (y + 4)(y - 10) = 0$$

$x + 3 = 0$		$x - 9 = 0$		$y + 4 = 0$		$y - 10 = 0$
$x = -3$	*or*	$x = 9$		$y = -4$	*or*	$y = 10$

The maximum possible value of $x + y = 9 + 10 = 19$.

10. **$x = \{1, 9\}$:**

$$x^2 - 10x + 25 = 16$$
$$x^2 - 10x + 9 = 0$$
$$(x - 9)(x - 1) = 0$$

$x - 9 = 0$		$x - 1 = 0$
$x = 9$	*or*	$x = 1$

11. **(D):** First, factor the equation in the common information:

$$x^2 - 2x - 15 = 0 \rightarrow (x - 5)(x + 3) = 0$$
$$x = 5 \text{ or } x = -3$$

$$x^2 - 2x - 15 = 0$$

Quantity A	**Quantity B**
$x = 5 \text{ or } -3$	1

The value of x could be greater than or less than 1. **The relationship cannot be determined.**

12. **(C):** First, factor the equation in the common information:

$$x^2 - 12x + 36 = 0 \rightarrow (x-6)(x-6) = 0$$
$$x = 6$$

$$x^2 - 12x + 36 = 0$$

Quantity A	**Quantity B**
$x = 6$	6

The two quantities are equal.

13. **(A):** Expand the expressions in both columns:

$$xy > 0$$

Quantity A	**Quantity B**
$(x+y)^2 =$	$(x-y)^2 =$
$x^2 + 2xy + y^2$	$x^2 - 2xy + y^2$

Now subtract $x^2 + y^2$ from both columns:

$$xy > 0$$

Quantity A	**Quantity B**
$x^2 + 2xy + y^2$	$x^2 - 2xy + y^2$
$-(x^2 \quad + \quad y^2)$	$-(x^2 \quad + \quad y^2)$
$2xy$	$-2xy$

Because xy is positive, Quantity A will be positive, regardless of the values of x and y. Similarly, Quantity B will always be negative, regardless of the values of x and y.

Quantity A is greater.

Chapter 4
of
Algebra

Inequalities &
Absolute Value

In This Chapter...

Chapter 4
Inequalities & Absolute Value

Inequalities

Earlier you explored how to solve equations. Now look at how you can solve *inequalities*.

Inequalities are expressions that use <, >, ≤, or ≥ to describe the relationship between two values.

Examples of inequalities:

$$5 > 4 \qquad y \leq 7 \qquad x < 5 \qquad 2x + 3 \geq 0$$

The table below illustrates how the various inequality symbols are translated. Notice that when inequalities are translated, you read from left to right:

$x < y$	x is less than y.	
$x > y$	x is greater than y.	
$x \leq y$	x is less than or equal to y.	x is at most y.
$x \geq y$	x is greater than or equal to y.	x is at least y.

You can also have two inequalities in one statement (sometimes called **compound inequalities**):

$9 < g < 200$	9 is less than g, and g is less than 200.
$-3 < y \leq 5$	−3 is less than y, and y is less than or equal to 5.
$7 \geq x > 2$	7 is greater than or equal to x, and x is greater than 2.

To visualize an inequality, it is helpful to represent it on a number line:

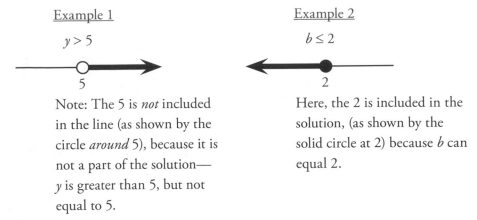

Example 1

$y > 5$

Note: The 5 is *not* included in the line (as shown by the circle *around* 5), because it is not a part of the solution— y is greater than 5, but not equal to 5.

Example 2

$b \leq 2$

Here, the 2 is included in the solution, (as shown by the solid circle at 2) because b can equal 2.

Visually, any number covered by the black arrow will make the inequality true and so is a possible solution to the inequality. Conversely, any number not covered by the black arrow will make the inequality untrue and is not a solution.

Check Your Skills

Represent the following equations on the number line provided.

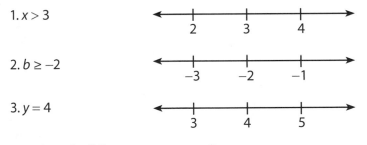

1. $x > 3$

2. $b \geq -2$

3. $y = 4$

Translate the following into inequality statements.

4. z is greater than v.
5. The total amount is greater than $2,000.

Answers can be found on page 99.

Solving Inequalities

What does it mean to "solve an inequality"?

You may be asking yourself, "I know what it means to solve an equation (such as $x = 2$), but what does it mean to solve an inequality?" Essentially, the principle is the same.

A solution is a number that makes an equation or inequality true. When you plug a solution back into the original equation or inequality, you get a *true statement*. This idea works the same for both equations and inequalities.

MANHATTAN
PREP

However, equations have only one, or just a few, values as solutions, but inequalities give a whole *range* of values as solutions—way too many to list individually.

Here's an example to help illustrate:

Equation: $x + 3 = 8$

The solution to $x + 3 = 8$ is $x = 5$.
5 is the *only* number that will make the equation true.

Plug back in to check:
$5 + 3 = 8$. True.

Inequality: $x + 3 < 8$

The solution to $x + 3 < 8$ is $x < 5$. Now, 5 itself is not a solution because $5 + 3 < 8$ is not a true statement. But, 4 is a solution because $4 + 3 < 8$ is true. For that matter, 4.99, 3, 2, 2.87, −5, and −100 are all also solutions. And the list goes on. Whichever of the correct answers you plug in, you need to arrive at something that looks like:

(Any number less than 5) + 3 < 8. True.

Check Your Skills

6. Which of the following numbers are solutions to the inequality $x < 10$?

Indicate <u>all</u> that apply.

- [A] −3
- [B] 2.5
- [C] −3/2
- [D] 9.999

Answer can be found on page 99.

Cleaning Up Inequalities

As with equations, your objective is to isolate the variable on one side of the inequality. When the variable is by itself, it is easiest to see what the solution (or range of solutions) really is. Although $2x + 6 < 12$ and $x < 3$ provide the same information (the second inequality is a simplified form of the first), you understand the full range of solutions much more easily when you look at the second inequality, which literally tells you that "x is less than 3."

Fortunately, the similarities between equations and inequalities don't end there—the techniques you will be using to clean up inequalities are the same that you used to clean up equations. (One important difference will be discussed shortly.)

Inequality Addition and Subtraction

If you were told that $x = 5$, what would $x + 3$ equal? $x + 3 = (5) + 3$, or $x + 3 = 8$. In other words, if you add the same number to both sides of an equation, the equation is still true.

The same holds true for inequalities. If you add or subtract the same number from both sides of an inequality, the inequality remains true:

Example 1

$a - 4 > 6$

$+4 \quad +4$

$a \qquad > 10$

Example 2

$y + 7 < 3$

$-7 \quad -7$

$y \qquad < -4$

You can also add or subtract variables from both sides of an inequality. There is no difference between adding/subtracting numbers and adding/subtracting variables:

$$3 - y > 0$$
$$+y \quad +y$$
$$3 \quad > y$$

Check Your Skills

Isolate the variable in the following inequalities.

7. $x - 6 < 13$

8. $y + 11 \geq -13$

9. $x + 7 > 7$

Answers can be found on page 99.

Inequality Multiplication and Division

You can also use multiplication and division to isolate the variables, as long as you recognize a very important distinction. *If you multiply or divide by a negative number, you must switch the direction of the inequality sign.* If you are multiplying or dividing by a positive number, the direction of the sign stays the same.

Here are a couple of examples to illustrate.

Multiplying or dividing by a *positive* number—the sign stays the same.

Example 1

$2x > 10$

$2x/2 > 10/2$ Divide each side by 2

$x > 5$

Example 2

$z/3 \le 2$

$z/3 \times (3) \le 2 \times (3)$ Multiply each side by 3

$z \le 6$

In both instances, the sign remains the same because you are multiplying or dividing by a positive number.

Multiplying or dividing by a *negative* number—switch the sign!

Example 1

$-2x > 10$

$-2x/-2 > 10/-2$ Divide each side by −2
                         Switch the sign!

$x < -5$

Example 2

$-4b \ge -8$

$-4b/-4 \ge -8/-4$ Divide each side by −4
                          Flip the inequality sign!

$b \le 2$

Why do you do this? Take a look at the following example that illustrates why you need to switch the signs when multiplying or dividing by a negative number:

Start with a TRUE Statement: 5 < 7			
Incorrect if you *don't* switch		**Switch the sign—Correct!**	
$(-1) \times 5 < (-1) \times 7$	Multiply both sides by −1	$(-1) \times 5 < (-1) \times 7$	Multiply both sides by −1 AND switch the sign!
$-5 < -7$?!?	NOT TRUE!	$-5 > -7$	STILL TRUE

In each case, you begin with a true inequality statement, 5 < 7, and then multiply by −1. You see that you have to switch the sign in order for the inequality statement to remain true.

What about multiplying or dividing an inequality by a *variable?* The short answer is…**try not to do it!** The issue is that you don't know the sign of the "hidden number" that the variable represents. If the variable logically can't be negative (e.g., it counts people or measures a length), then you can go ahead and multiply or divide.

If the variable must be negative, then you are also free to multiply or divide—just remember to flip the sign. However, if you don't know whether the variable is positive or negative, try to work through the problem with the inequality as is. (If the problem is a Quantitative Comparison, consider whether not knowing the sign of the variable you want to multiply or divide by means that the answer is (D)!)

Check Your Skills

Isolate the variable in each equation.

10. $x + 3 \geq -2$
11. $-2y < 8$
12. $a + 4 \geq 2a$

Answers can be found on page 99.

Absolute Value—Distance on the Number Line

4

The GRE adds another level of difficulty to equations and inequalities in the form of *absolute value*.

The "absolute value" of a number describes how far that number is away from 0. It is the distance between that number and 0 on a number line. The symbol for absolute value is |number|. For instance, the absolute value of −5 is written as |−5|.

Example 1: The absolute value of 5 is 5:

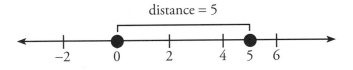

Example 2: The absolute value of −5 is also 5:

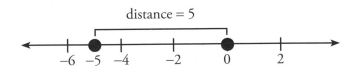

When you face an expression like |4 − 7|, treat the absolute value symbol like parentheses. Solve the arithmetic problem inside first, and then find the absolute value of the answer. In this case, $4 - 7 = -3$, and −3 is 3 units from zero, so $|4 - 7| = |-3| = 3$.

Check Your Skills

Mark the following expressions as True or False.

13. $|3| = 3$
14. $|-3| = -3$
15. $|3| = -3$
16. $|-3| = 3$
17. $|3 - 6| = 3$
18. $|6 - 3| = -3$

Answers can be found on pages 99–100.

Solving Absolute Value Equations

On the GRE, some absolute value equations place a variable inside the absolute value signs:

Example: $|y| = 3$

What's the trap here? The trap is that there are two numbers, 3 and −3, that are 3 units away from 0. That means both of these numbers could be possible values for y. So how do you figure that out? Here, you can't. All you can say is that y could be either the positive value or the negative value; y is either 3 or −3.

When there is a variable inside an absolute value, you should look for the variable to have two possible values. Although you will not always be able to determine which of the two is the correct value, it is important to be able to find both values. Following is a step-by-step process for finding all solutions to an equation that contains a variable inside an absolute value:

$|y| = 3$

Step 1: Isolate the absolute value expression on one side of the equation. In this case, the absolute value expression is already isolated.

$+(y) = 3$ or $-(y) = 3$

Step 2: Take what's inside the absolute value sign and set up two equations. The first sets the positive value equal to the other side of the equation, and the second sets the negative value equal to the other side.

$y = 3$ or $-y = 3$
$y = 3$ or $y = -3$

Step 3: Solve both equations.
Note: There are two possible values for y.

Sometimes people take a shortcut and go right to "y equals plus or minus 3." This shortcut works as long as the absolute value expression is by itself on one side of the equation.

Here's a slightly more difficult problem, using the same technique:

Example: $6 \times |2x + 4| = 30$

To solve this, you can use the same approach:

$$6 \times |2x + 4| = 30$$

$$|2x + 4| = 5$$ Step 1: Isolate the absolute value expression on one side of the equation or inequality.

$(2x + 4) = 5$ or $-(2x + 4) = 5$ Step 2: Set up two equations—the positive and the negative
$2x + 4 = 5$ or $-2x - 4 = 5$ values are set equal to the other side.

$2x = 1$ or $-2x = 9$ Step 3: Solve both equations/inequalities.

$x = 1/2$ or $x = -9/2$ Note: There are two possible values for x.

Check Your Skills

Solve the following equations with absolute values in them.

19. $|a| = 6$
20. $|x + 2| = 5$
21. $|3y - 4| = 17$
22. $4|x + 1/2| = 18$

Answers can be found on page 100.

Putting Them Together: Inequalities and Absolute Values

Some problems on the GRE include both inequalities and absolute values. You can solve these problems by combining what you have learned about solving inequalities with what you have learned about solving absolute values:

Example 1: $|x| \geq 4$

Even though you're now dealing with an inequality, and not an equal sign, the basic process is the same. The absolute value is already isolated on one side, so now you need to set up your two equations or, in this case, inequalities. The first inequality replaces the absolute value with the *positive* of what's inside, and the second replaces the absolute value with the *negative* of what's inside:

$+ (x) \geq 4$ or $- (x) \geq 4$

Now that you have your two equations, isolate the variable in each equation:

$+ (x) \geq 4$	$- (x) \geq 4$
$x \geq 4$	$-x \geq 4$ Divide by -1.
	$x \leq -4$ Remember to flip the sign when dividing by a negative.

So the two solutions to the original equation are $x \geq 4$ and $x \leq -4$. Here it is represented on a number line:

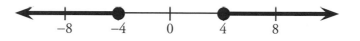

As before, any number that is covered by the black arrow will make the inequality true. Because of the absolute value, there are now two arrows instead of one, but nothing else has changed. Any number to the left of -4 will make the inequality true, as will any number to the right of 4.

Looking back at the inequality $|x| \geq 4$, you can now interpret it in terms of distance. $|x| \geq 4$ means "x is at least 4 units away from zero, in either direction." The black arrows indicate all numbers for which that statement is true.

4

Example 2: $|x + 3| < 5$

Once again, the absolute value is already isolated on one side, so now you need to set up the two inequalities. The first inequality replaces the absolute value with the *positive* of what's inside, and the second replaces the absolute value with the *negative* of what's inside:

$+ (x + 3) < 5$ and $- (x + 3) < 5$

Next, isolate the variable in each equation:

$x + 3 < 5$	$-x - 3 < 5$
$x < 2$	$-x < 8$
	$x > -8$

So the two equations are $x < 2$ and $x > -8$. But now something curious happens if those two equations are plotted on the number line:

It seems like every number should be a solution to the equation. But if you start testing numbers, that isn't the case. Test out $x = 5$, for example. Is $|5 + 3| < 5$? No, it isn't. As it turns out, the only numbers that make the original inequality true are those that are true for *both* inequalities. Really, your number line should look like this:

In the first example, it was the case that *x* could be greater than or equal to 4 *or* less than or equal to −4. For this example, however, it seems to make more sense to say that *x* is greater than −8 *and* less than 2.

The inequality you just graphed means "($x + 3$) is less than 5 units away from from zero, in either direction." The shaded segment indicates all numbers *x* for which this is true. As the inequalities become more complicated, don't worry about interpreting their meaning—simply solve them algebraically!

To summarize, when representing inequalities on the number line, absolute value expressions where variables are *greater than some quantity* will show up *as two ranges in opposite directions* (or "double arrows"); however, absolute value expressions where variables are *less than some quantity* will show up *as a single range* (or "line segment").

Check Your Skills

23. $|x + 1| > 2$
24. $|-x - 4| \geq 8$
25. $|x - 7| < 9$

Answers can be found on pages 100–101.

Manipulating Compound Inequalities

Sometimes a problem with compound inequalities will require you to manipulate the inequalities in order to solve the problem. You can perform operations on a compound inequality as long as you remember to perform those operations on **every term** in the inequality, not just the outside terms. For example:

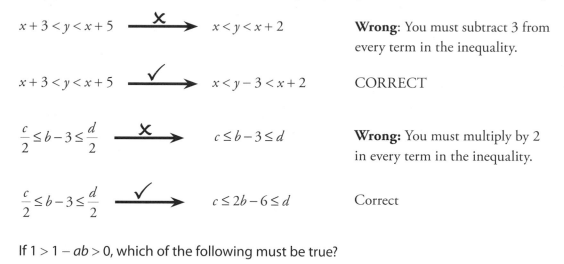

$x + 3 < y < x + 5 \xrightarrow{\ \times\ } x < y < x + 2$ **Wrong**: You must subtract 3 from every term in the inequality.

$x + 3 < y < x + 5 \xrightarrow{\ \checkmark\ } x < y - 3 < x + 2$ CORRECT

$\dfrac{c}{2} \le b - 3 \le \dfrac{d}{2} \xrightarrow{\ \times\ } c \le b - 3 \le d$ **Wrong**: You must multiply by 2 in every term in the inequality.

$\dfrac{c}{2} \le b - 3 \le \dfrac{d}{2} \xrightarrow{\ \checkmark\ } c \le 2b - 6 \le d$ Correct

If $1 > 1 - ab > 0$, which of the following must be true?

Indicate <u>all</u> that apply.

A $\dfrac{a}{b} > 0$

B $\dfrac{a}{b} < 1$

C $ab < 1$

You can manipulate the original compound inequality as follows, making sure to perform each manipulation on every term:

$1 > 1 - ab > 0$
$0 > \ -ab > -1$ Subtract 1 from all three terms.
$0 < \ \ \ ab < 1$ Multiply all three terms by -1 and flip the inequality signs.

Therefore, you know that $0 < ab < 1$. This tells you that ab is positive, so $\dfrac{a}{b}$ must be positive (a and b have the same sign). Therefore, (A) must be true. However, you do not know whether $\dfrac{a}{b} < 1$, so (B) is not necessarily true. But you do know that ab must be less than 1, so (C) must be true. Therefore, the correct answers are (A) and (C).

Check Your Skills

26. Find the range of values for x if $-7 < 3 - 2x < 9$.

Answer can be found on page 101.

Using Extreme Values

One effective technique for solving GRE inequality problems is to focus on the **Extreme Values** of a given inequality. This is particularly helpful when solving the following types of inequality problems:

1. Problems with multiple inequalities where the question involves the potential range of values for variables in the problem
2. Problems involving both equations and inequalities

Inequalities with Ranges

Whenever a question asks about the possible range of values for a problem, consider using Extreme Values:

> If $0 \leq x \leq 3$ and $y < 8$, which of the following could NOT be the value of xy?
>
>   (A) 0   (B) 8   (C) 12   (D) 16   (E) 24

To solve this problem, consider the **Extreme Values** of each variable:

Extreme Values for x	**Extreme Values for y**
The lowest value for x is **0**.	The lowest value for y is negative infinity.
The highest value for x is **3**.	The highest value for y is **less than 8**.

(Since y cannot be 8, this upper limit is termed "less than 8" or "LT8" for shorthand.)

What is the lowest value for xy? Plug in the lowest values for both x and y. In this problem, y has no lower limit, so there is no lower limit to xy.

What is the highest value for xy? Plug in the highest values for both x and y. In this problem, the highest value for x is **3**, and the highest value for y is **LT8**.

Multiplying these two extremes together yields: $3 \times \text{LT8} = \text{LT24}$. Notice that you can multiply LT8 by another number (as long as that other number is positive) just as though it were 8. You just have to remember to include the "LT" tag on the result.

Because the upper extreme for xy is less than 24, xy CANNOT be 24, and the answer is **(E)**.

Notice that you would run into trouble if x did not have to be non-negative. Consider this slight variation:

> If $-1 \leq x \leq 3$ and $y < 8$, what is the possible range of values for xy?

Because x could be negative and because y could be a very negative number, there is no longer an upper extreme on xy. For example, if $x = -1$ and $y = -1,000$, then $xy = 1,000$. Obviously, even greater positive

results are possible for xy if both x and y are very negative. Likewise, since x can be positive and y can be infinitely negative, xy can be infinitely negative. Therefore, xy can equal any number.

Check Your Skills

27. If $-4 < a < 4$ and $-2 < b < -1$, which of the following could NOT be the value of ab?

    (A) −3
    (B)   0
    (C)   4
    (D)   6
    (E)   9

Answer can be found on page 101.

Optimization Problems

Related to extreme values are problems involving optimization: specifically, minimization or maximization problems. In these problems, you need to **focus on the largest and smallest possible values for each of the variables**, as some combination of them will usually lead to the largest or smallest possible result:

If $-7 \leq a \leq 6$ and $-7 \leq b \leq 8$, what is the maximum possible value for ab?

Once again, you are looking for a maximum possible value, this time for ab. You need to test the extreme values for a and for b to determine which combinations of extreme values will maximize ab:

Extreme Values for a

The lowest value for a is −7.
The highest value for a is 6.

Extreme Values for b

The lowest value for b is −7.
The highest value for b is 8.

Now consider the different extreme value scenarios for a, b, and ab:

a		b		ab
Min	−7	Min	−7	$(-7) \times (-7) = \mathbf{49}$
Min	−7	Max	8	$(-7) \times 8 = -56$
Max	6	Min	−7	$6 \times (-7) = -42$
Max	6	Max	8	$6 \times 8 = 48$

This time, ab is maximized when you take the *negative* extreme values for both a and b, resulting in $ab = 49$. Notice that you could have focused right away on the first and fourth scenarios, because they are the only scenarios that produce positive products.

If $-4 \leq m \leq 7$ and $-3 < n < 10$, what is the maximum possible integer value for $m - n$?

Again, you are looking for a maximum possible value, this time for $m - n$. You need to test the extreme values for m and for n to determine which combinations of extreme values will maximize $m - n$:

Extreme Values for m	**Extreme Values for n**
The lowest value for m is -4.	The lowest value for n is greater than -3.
The highest value for m is 7.	The highest value for n is less than 10.

Now consider the different extreme value scenarios for m, n, and $m - n$:

m		n		$m - n$
Min	-4	Min	GT(-3)	$(-4) -$ GT(-3) $=$ LT(-1)
Min	-4	Max	LT10	$(-4) -$ LT10 $=$ GT(-14)
Max	7	Min	**GT(-3)**	**7 $-$ GT(-3) $=$ LT10**
Max	7	Max	LT10	$7 -$ LT10 $=$ GT(-3)

Thus, $m - n$ is maximized when you take the *maximum* extreme for m and the *minimum* extreme for n, resulting in $m - n =$ less than 10. The largest integer less than 10 is 9, so the correct answer is $\boldsymbol{m - n =}$ **9**. Look at another, slightly different, problem:

If $x \geq 4 + (z + 1)^2$, what is the minimum possible value for x?

The key to this type of problem—where you need to maximize or minimize when one of the variables has an even exponent—is to recognize that the squared term will be minimized when it is set equal to 0. Therefore, you need to set $(z + 1)^2$ equal to 0:

$x \geq 4 =$ (at least 0)

Therefore, 4 is the minimum possible value for x.

Check Your Skills

28. If $-1 \leq a \leq 4$ and $-6 \leq b \leq -2$, what is the minimum value for $b - a$?
29. If $(x + 2)^2 \leq 2 - y$, what is the maximum possible value for y?

Answers can be found on page 101.

Summary of Inequality Techniques

Many topics in inequalities have been covered. Here is a quick recap of "Dos and Don'ts" when working with inequalities:

Dos	Don'ts
• DO think about inequalities as ranges on a number line.	• DON'T forget to flip the inequality sign if you multiply or divide both sides of an inequality by a negative number.
• DO treat inequalities like equations when adding or subtracting terms, or when multiplying/dividing by a positive number on both sides of the inequality.	• DON'T multiply or divide an inequality by a variable unless you know the sign of the variable.
• DO use extreme values to solve inequality range problems, problems containing both inequalities and equations, and many optimization problems.	• DON'T forget to perform operations on every expression when manipulating a compound inequality.
• DO set terms with even exponents equal to 0 when trying to solve minimization problems.	

Check Your Skills Answer Key

1.

2.

3.

4. $z > v$

5. Let a = total amount.

   $a > \$2{,}000$

6. **(A)**, **(B)**, **(C)**, **(D)**: All of these numbers are to the left of 10 on the number line.

7. $x - 6 < 13$
   $x < 19$

8. $y + 11 \geq -13$
   $y \geq -24$

9. $x + 7 > 7$
   $x > 0$

10. $x + 3 \geq -2$
    $x \geq -5$

11. $-2y < 8$
    $y > -4$

12. $a + 4 \geq 2a$
    $4 \geq a$

13. **True**

14. **False** *(Note that absolute value is always positive!)*

15. **False**

16. **True**

17. **True** ($|3 - 6| = |-3| = 3$)

18. **False**

19. $|a| = 6$

$$a = 6 \qquad \text{or} \qquad a = -6$$

20. $x = 3$ **or** -7: $|x + 2| = 5$

$+ (x + 2) = 5$	or	$-(x + 2) = 5$
$x + 2 = 5$	or	$-x - 2 = 5$
$x = 3$	or	$-x = 7$
		$x = -7$

21. $y = 7$ **or** $-13/3$: $|3y - 4| = 17$

$+ (3y - 4) = 17$	or	$-(3y - 4) = 17$
$3y - 4 = 17$	or	$-3y + 4 = 17$
$3y = 21$	or	$-3y = 13$
$y = 7$	or	$y = -13/3$

22. $x = 4$ **or** -5: or $4|x + 1/2| = 18$

$+ (x + 1/2) = 4 \ 1/2$	or	$-(x + 1/2) = 4 \ 1/2$
$x + 1/2 = 4 \ 1/2$	or	$-x - 1/2 = 4 \ 1/2$
$x = 4$	or	$-x = 5$
		$x = -5$

23. $|x + 1| > 2$

$+ (x + 1) > 2$	or	$-(x + 1) > 2$
$x + 1 > 2$	or	$-x - 1 > 2$
$x > 1$	or	$-x > 3$
		$x < -3$

$$x < -3 \qquad \textbf{or} \qquad x > 1$$

24. $|-x - 4| \geq 8$

$+ (-x - 4) \geq 8$	or	$-(-x - 4) \geq 8$
$-x - 4 \geq 8$	or	$x + 4 \geq 8$
$-x \geq 12$	or	$x \geq 4$
$x \leq -12$		

$$x \leq -12 \qquad \textbf{or} \qquad x \geq 4$$

MANHATTAN
PREP

25. $|x - 7| < 9$

$+(x - 7) < 9$	or	$-(x - 7) < 9$
$x - 7 < 9$	or	$-x + 7 < 9$
$x < 16$	or	$-x < 2$
		$x > -2$

$x > -2$ and $x < 16$, $-2 < x < 16$

26. $-3 < x < 5$: $-7 < 3 - 2x < 9$

$-10 < -2x < 6$ Subtract 3 from all three terms.

$5 > x > -3$ Divide all three terms by -2, and flip the inequality signs.

or $-3 < x < 5$

27. **(E):** Extreme values for a are greater than -4 and less than 4. Extreme values for b are greater than -2 and less than -1.

Note that a can be positive, zero, or negative, while b can only be negative, so ab can be positive, zero, and negative.

The most negative ab can be is (less positive than 4) × (less negative than -2) = less negative than -8.
The most positive ab can be is (less negative than -4) × (less negative than -2) = less positive than 8.

28. **-10:**

a	b	$b - a$
-1	-6	$-6 - (-1) = -5$
-1	-2	$-2 - (-1) = -1$
4	-6	$-6 - 4 = -10$
4	-2	$-2 - 4 = -6$

29. **2:** $(x + 2)^2 \leq 2 - y$

$y + (x + 2)^2 \leq 2$ Add y to both sides.

$y \leq 2 - (x + 2)^2$ Subtract $(x + 2)^2$ from both sides.

Note that y is maximized when $(x + 2)^2$ is minimized. The smallest possible value for $(x + 2)^2$ is 0, when $x = -2$. When $(x + 2)^2 = 0$, $y = 2$.

Problem Set

1. $4x - 12 \geq x + 9$

Quantity A	**Quantity B**
x	6

2. Which of the following is equivalent to $-3x + 7 \leq 2x + 32$?

 (A) $x \geq -5$ (B) $x \geq 5$ (C) $x \leq 5$ (D) $x \leq -5$

3. If $G^2 < G$, which of the following could be G?

 (A) 1   (B) $\dfrac{23}{7}$ (C) $\dfrac{7}{23}$ (D) -4 (E) -2

4. If $|A| > 19$, which of the following *cannot* be equal to A?

 (A) 26   (B) 22   (C) 18   (D) -20 (E) -24

5. If $B^3A < 0$ and $A > 0$, which of the following must be negative?

 (A) AB (B) B^2A (C) B^4 (D) $\dfrac{A}{B^2}$ (E) $-\dfrac{B}{A}$

6. $|2x - 5| \leq 7$

Quantity A	**Quantity B**
x	3

7. $1 \leq x \leq 5$ and $1 \geq y \geq -2$

Quantity A	**Quantity B**
xy	-10

8. $x = 4$

Quantity A	**Quantity B**
$|2 - x|$	2

Solutions

1. **(A):** $4x - 12 \geq x + 9$ If $x \geq 7$, then $x > 6$.

   $3x \geq 21$

   $x \geq 7$

2. **(A):** $-3x + 7 \leq 2x + 32$

   $-5x \leq 25$

   $x \geq -5$ When you divide by a negative number, you must
   reverse the direction of the inequality symbol.

3. **(C):** If $G^2 < G$, then G must be positive (since G^2 will never be negative), and G must be less than 1, because otherwise, $G^2 > G$. Thus, $0 < G < 1$. You can eliminate choices (D) and (E), since they violate the condition that G be positive. Then test choice (A): 1 is not less than 1, so you can eliminate (A). Choice (B) is greater than 1, so only choice (C) satisfies the inequality.

4. **(C):** If $|A| > 19$, then $A > 19$ OR $A < -19$. The only answer choice that does not satisfy either of these inequalities is choice (C), 18.

5. **(A):** If A is positive, B^3 must be negative. Therefore, B must be negative. If A is positive and B is negative, the product AB must be negative.

6. **(D):** To evaluate the absolute value, set up two equations and isolate x:

$+ (2x - 5) \leq 7$	and	$-(2x - 5) \leq 7$
$2x - 5 \leq 7$		$-2x + 5 \leq 7$
$2x \leq 12$		$-2x \leq 2$
$x \leq 6$		$x \geq -1$

Combine the information from the two equations:

$$|2x - 5| \leq 7$$

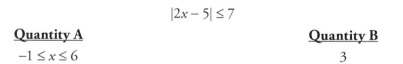

Quantity A   **Quantity B**

$-1 \leq x \leq 6$ 3

There are possible values of x greater than *and* less than 3. **The relationship cannot be determined.**

7. **(D):** To find the minimum and maximum values of xy, test the boundaries of x and y:

x		y		xy
Min	1	Min	-2	$(1) \times (-2) = -2$
Min	1	Max	1	$(1) \times (1) = 1$
Max	5	Min	-2	$(5) \times (-2) = -10$
Max	5	Max	1	$(5) \times (1) = 5$

Combine the information from the chart to show the range of xy:

$$1 \leq x \leq 5 \text{ and } 1 \geq y \geq -2$$

Quantity A	**Quantity B**
$-10 \leq xy \leq 5$	-10

Quantity A can be either greater than or equal to -10. **The relationship cannot be determined.**

8. **(C):** Plug in 4 for x in Quantity A.

$$x = 4$$

Quantity A	**Quantity B**
$\lvert 2 - x \rvert =$	2
$\lvert 2 - (4) \rvert = \lvert -2 \rvert = 2$	

The two quantities are equal.

Chapter 5
of
Algebra

Formulas & Functions

In This Chapter. . .

Chapter 5
Formulas & Functions

Plug In Formulas

The most basic GRE formula problems provide you with a formula and ask you to solve for one of the variables in the formula by plugging in given values for the other variables. For example:

> The formula for determining an individual's comedic aptitude, C, on a given day is defined as $\dfrac{QL}{J}$, where J represents the number of jokes told, Q represents the overall joke quality on a scale of 1 to 10, and L represents the number of individual laughs generated. If Nicole told 12 jokes, generated 18 laughs, and earned a comedic aptitude of 10.5, what was the overall quality of her jokes?

Solving this problem simply involves plugging the given values into the formula in order to solve for the unknown variable Q:

$$C = \frac{QL}{J} \rightarrow 10.5 = \frac{18Q}{12} \rightarrow 10.5(12) = 18Q \rightarrow Q = \frac{10.5(12)}{18} \rightarrow Q = 7$$

The quality of Nicole's jokes was rated a 7.

Notice that you will typically have to do some rearrangement after plugging in the numbers, in order to isolate the desired unknown. The actual computations are not complex. What makes formula problems tricky is the unfamiliarity of the given formula, which may seem to come from "out of the blue." Do not be intimidated. Simply write the equation down, plug in the numbers carefully, and solve for the required unknown.

Be sure to write the formula as a part of an equation. For instance, do not just write "$\dfrac{QL}{J}$" on your paper. Rather, write "$C = \dfrac{QL}{J}$." Look for language such as "is defined as" to identify what equals what.

<u>Check Your Skills</u>

1. For a certain cake, the baking time in minutes is defined as $\dfrac{Vk}{T}$, where V is the volume of the cake in inches³, T is the oven temperature in degrees Fahrenheit, and k is a constant. If the baking time was 30 minutes at 350 degrees Fahrenheit for a 150 inches³ cake, what is the value of constant k?

Answer can be found on page 121.

Strange Symbol Formulas

Another type of GRE formula problem involves the use of strange symbols. In these problems, the GRE introduces an arbitrary symbol, which defines a certain procedure. These problems may look confusing because of the unfamiliar symbols. However, the symbol is *irrelevant*. All that is important is that you carefully follow each step in the procedure that the symbol indicates.

A technique that can be helpful is to break the operations down one-by-one and say them aloud (or in your head)—to "hear" them explicitly. Here are some examples:

<u>Formula Definition</u>	<u>Step-by-Step Breakdown</u>
$x \heartsuit y = x^2 + y^2 - xy$	"The first number squared, plus the second number squared, minus the product of the two …"
$s \bigcirc t = (s - 2)(t + 2)$	"Two less than the first number times two more than the second number …"
$\boxed{x}$ is defined as the product of all integers smaller than x but greater than 0 …	"… x minus 1, times x minus 2, times x minus 3 … Aha! So this is $(x - 1)$ factorial!"

Notice that it can be helpful to refer to the variables as "the first number," "the second number," and so on. In this way, you use the physical position of the numbers to keep them straight in relation to the strange symbol.

Now that you have interpreted the formula step-by-step and can understand what it means, you can calculate a solution for the formula with actual numbers. Consider the following example:

$$W \psi F = \left(\sqrt{W}\right)^F \text{ for all integers } W \text{ and } F. \text{ What is } 4 \ \psi \ 3?$$

The symbol ψ between two numbers signals the following procedure: take the square root of the FIRST number and then raise that value to the power of the *second* number:

$$4 \ \psi \ 3 = \left(\sqrt{4}\right)^3 = 2^3 = 8$$

Watch out for symbols that *invert* the order of an operation. It is easy to automatically translate the function in a "left to right" manner even when that is *not* what the function specifies:

$$W \Phi F = \left(\sqrt{F}\right)^W \text{ for all integers } W \text{ and } F. \text{ What is } 4 \Phi 9?$$

It would be easy in this example to mistakenly calculate the formula in the same way as the first example. However, notice that the order of the operation is *reversed*—you need to take the square root of the *second* number, raised to the power of the *first* number:

$$4 \Phi 9 = \left(\sqrt{9}\right)^4 = 3^4 = 81$$

More challenging strange-symbol problems require you to use the given procedure more than once. For example:

$$A \Phi B = \left(\sqrt{B}\right)^A \text{ for all integers } A \text{ and } B. \text{ What is } 2 \Phi (3 \Phi 16)?$$

Always perform the procedure inside the parentheses FIRST:

$$3 \Phi 16 = \left(\sqrt{16}\right)^3 = 4^3 = 64$$

Now you can rewrite the original formula as follows: $2 \Phi (3 \Phi 16) = 2 \Phi 64$.

Performing the procedure a second time yields the answer:

$$2 \Phi 64 = \left(\sqrt{64}\right)^2 = 8^2 = 64$$

Check Your Skills

2. $A \triangle B = A^B + B$ for all integers A and B. What is the value of $-2\triangle(3 \triangle 1)$?

3. $s \lambda t = \dfrac{t}{s} + \dfrac{s}{t}$ for all integers s and t. What is the value of $2\lambda16$?

Answers can be found on page 121.

Formulas with Unspecified Amounts

Some of the most challenging formula problems on the GRE are those that involve unspecified amounts. Typically, these questions focus on the increase or decrease in the value of a certain formula, given a change in the value of the variables. Just as with other GRE problems with unspecified amounts, solve these problems by picking numbers!

> If the length of the side of a cube decreases by two-thirds its original value, by what percent will the volume of the cube decrease?

First consider the formula involved here. The volume of a cube is defined by the formula $V = s^3$, where s represents the length of a side. Then pick a number for the length of the side of the cube.

Say the cube has a side of 3 units. Note that this is a "smart" number to pick because it is divisible by 3 (the denominator of two-thirds).

Then its volume equals $s^3 = 3 \times 3 \times 3 = 27$.

If the cube's side decreases by two-thirds, its new length is $3 - \dfrac{2}{3}(3) = 1$ unit.

Its new volume equals $s^3 = 1 \times 1 \times 1 = 1$.

You determine percent decrease as follows:

$$\frac{\text{change}}{\text{original}} = \frac{27 - 1}{27} = \frac{26}{27} \approx 0.963 = 96.3\% \text{ decrease}$$

Check Your Skills

4. When Tom moved to a new home, his distance to work decreased by 1/2 the original distance and the constant rate at which he travels to work increased by 1/3 the original rate. By what percent has the time it takes Tom to travel to work decreased?

Answer can be found on page 121.

Sequence Formulas: Direct and Recursive

The final type of GRE formula problem involves sequences. A sequence is a collection of numbers in a set order. The order of a given sequence is determined by a **rule**. Here are examples of sequence rules:

For all integers $n \geq 1$...

$A_n = 9n + 3$　　The nth term of this sequence is defined by the rule $9n + 3$, for integers $n \geq 1$. For example, the fourth term in this sequence is $9n + 3 = 9(4) + 3 = 39$. The first ten terms of the sequence are as follows:

　　　　　　　　12, 21, 30, 39, 48, 57, 66, 75, 84, 93
　　　　　　　　(notice that successive terms differ by 9)

$Q_n = n^2 + 4$　　The nth term of this sequence is defined by the rule $n^2 + 4$, for integers $n \geq 1$. For example, the first term in this sequence is $1^2 + 4 = 5$. The first ten terms of the sequence are as follows:

　　　　　　　　5, 8, 13, 20, 29, 40, 53, 68, 85, 104

In the above cases, each item of the sequence is defined as a function of n, the place in which the term occurs in the sequence. For example, the value of A_5 is a function of its being the 5th item in the sequence. This is a **direct** definition of a sequence formula.

The GRE also uses **recursive** formulas to define sequences. With **direct** formulas, the value of each item in a sequence is defined in terms of its item number in the sequence. With **recursive** formulas, each item of a sequence is defined in terms of the value of previous items in the sequence.

A recursive formula looks like this:

$$A_n = A_{n-1} + 9$$

This formula simply means "This term (A_n) equals the previous term (A_{n-1}) plus 9." It is shorthand for a series of specific relationships between successive terms:

$$A_2 = A_1 + 9$$
$$A_3 = A_2 + 9$$
$$A_4 = A_3 + 9, \text{ etc.}$$

Whenever you look at a recursive formula, *articulate its meaning in words in your mind*. If necessary, also write out one or two specific relationships that the recursive formula stands for. Think of a recursive formula as a "domino" relationship: if you know A_1, then you can find A_2, and then you can find A_3, then A_4, and so on for all the terms. You can also work backward: if you know A_4, then you can find A_3, A_2, and A_1. However, if you do not know the value of any one term, then you cannot calculate the value of any other. You need one domino to fall, so to speak, in order to knock down all the others.

Thus, to solve for the values of a recursive sequence, you need to be given the recursive rule and *also* the value of one of the items in the sequence. For example:

$$A_n = A_{n-1} + 9$$
$$A_1 = 12$$

In this example, A_n is defined in terms of the previous item, A_{n-1}. Recall the meaning of this recursive formula: This term equals the previous term plus 9. Because $A_1 = 12$, you can determine that $A_2 = A_1 + 9 = 12 + 9 = 21$. Therefore, $A_3 = 21 + 9 = 30$, $A_4 = 30 + 9 = 39$, and so on.

Because the first term is 12, this sequence is identical to the sequence defined by the direct definition, $A_n = 9n + 3$, given at the beginning of this section. Here is another example:

$$F_n = F_{n-1} + F_{n-2}$$
$$F_1 = 1, F_2 = 1$$
for all integers
$$n \geq 3$$

In this example, F_n is defined in terms of both the previous item, F_{n-1}, and the item prior to that, F_{n-2}. This recursive formula means "This term equals the previous term plus the term before that." Because $F_1 = 1$ and $F_2 = 1$, you can determine that $F_3 = F_1 + F_2 = 1 + 1 = 2$. Therefore, $F_4 = 2 + 1 = 3$, $F_5 = 3 + 2 = 5$, $F_6 = 5 + 3 = 8$, and so on. There is no simple direct rule for this sequence.

Check Your Skills

5. $S_n = 2n - 5$ for all integers $n \geq 1$. What is the 11th term of the sequence?

6. $B_n = (-1)^n \times n + 3$ for all integers $n \geq 1$. What is the 9th term of the sequence?

7. If $A_n = 2A_{n-1} + 3$ for all $n \geq 1$, and $A_4 = 45$, what is A_1?

Answers can be found on page 121.

Sequence Problems

For sequence problems on the GRE, you may be asked to do any of the following:

- Determine which answer choice corresponds to the correct *definition* (or *rule*) for a sequence (direct or recursive).
- Determine the value of a particular *item* in a sequence.
- Determine the sum or difference of a *set of items* in a sequence.

For simple linear sequences, in which the same number is added to any term to yield the next term, you can use the following alternative method—rather than find the rule or definition for the sequence, you can sometimes logically derive one item in the sequence based on the information given:

> **If each number in a sequence is three more than the previous number, and the sixth number is 32, what is the 100th number?**

Instead of finding the rule for this sequence, consider the following reasoning:

From the sixth term to the one hundredth term, there are 94 "jumps" of 3. Since $94 \times 3 = 282$, there is an increase of 282 from the sixth term to the one hundredth term:

$$32 + 282 = 314$$

Check Your Skills

8. If each number of a sequence is 4 more than the previous number, and the 3rd number in the sequence is 13, what is the 114th number in the sequence?

Answer can be found on page 122.

Sequences and Patterns

As has been discussed, sequence problems generally involve finding patterns among the *items in a sequence*, or the *definition/rule for the sequence*. Generally, for questions involving the sequence *items themselves*, the best approach involves writing down information (often in the form of an equation) for *specific items* in the sequence, and trying to find a *pattern* among these items.

> If $S_n = 3^n$, what is the units digit of S_{65}?

Clearly, you cannot be expected to multiply out 3^{65} on the GRE, even with a calculator. Therefore, you must look for a pattern in the powers of three.

$$3^1 = \quad 3$$
$$3^2 = \quad 9$$
$$3^3 = \quad 27$$
$$3^4 = \quad 81$$
$$3^5 = \quad 243$$
$$3^6 = \quad 729$$
$$3^7 = 2,187$$
$$3^8 = 6,561$$

You can see that the units digits of powers of 3 follow the pattern "3, 9, 7, 1" before repeating. The units digit of 3^{65} will thus be 3, because the 64th term will be "1" as 64 is divisible by 4 (and the pattern repeats every four terms).

As a side note, most sequences on the GRE are defined for integers $n \geq 1$. That is, sequence S_n almost always starts at S_1. Occasionally, a sequence might start at S_0, but in that case, you will be told that n could equal 0.

Check Your Skills

9. If $A_n = 7^n - 1$, what is the units digit of A_{33}?

Answer can be found on page 122.

Functions

Functions are very much like the "magic boxes" you may have learned about in elementary school. For example:

> You put a 2 into the magic box, and a 7 comes out. You put a 3 into the magic box, and a 9 comes out. You put a 4 into the magic box, and an 11 comes out. What is the magic box doing to your number?

There are many possible ways to describe what the magic box is doing to your number. One possibility is as follows: The magic box is doubling your number and adding 3:

$$2(2) + 3 = 7 \qquad\qquad 2(3) + 3 = 9 \qquad\qquad 2(4) + 3 = 11$$

Assuming that this is the case (it is possible that the magic box is actually doing something different to your number), this description would yield the following "rule" for this magic box: $2x + 3$. This rule can be written in function form as:

$$f(x) = 2x + 3$$

The function f represents the "rule" that the magic box is using to transform your number. Again, this rule may or may not be the "true" rule for the magic box. That is, if you put more numbers into the box and watch what numbers emerge, this rule may or may not hold. It is never possible to generalize a rule only by using specific cases.

Nevertheless, the magic box analogy is a helpful way to conceptualize a function as a rule built on an independent variable. The value of a function changes as the value of the independent variable changes. In other words, the value of a function is dependent on the value of the independent variable. Examples of functions include:

$$f(x) = 4x^2 - 11$$

The value of the function, f, is *dependent* on the *independent* variable, x.

$$g(t) = t^3 + \sqrt{t} - \frac{2t}{5}$$

The value of the function, g, is *dependent* on the *independent* variable, t.

Think of functions as consisting of an "input" variable (the number you put into the magic box), and a corresponding "output" value (the number that comes out of the box). The function is simply the rule that turns the "input" variable into the "output" variable.

By the way, the expression $f(x)$ is pronounced "f of x", not "fx." It does not mean "f times x"! The letter f does not stand for a variable; rather, it stands for the rule that dictates how the input x changes into the output $f(x)$.

The "domain" of a function indicates the possible inputs. The "range" of a function indicates the possible outputs. For instance, the function $f(x) = x^2$ can take any input but never produces a negative number. So the domain is all numbers, but the range is $f(x) \geq 0$.

Numerical Substitution

This is the most basic type of function problem. Input the numerical value (say, 5) in place of the independent variable (x) to determine the value of the function:

If $f(x) = x^2 - 2$, what is the value of $f(5)$?

In this problem, you are given a rule for $f(x)$: square x and subtract 2. Then, you are asked to apply this rule to the number 5. Square 5 and subtract 2 from the result:

$$f(5) = (5)^2 - 2 = 25 - 2 = 23$$

Variable Substitution

This type of problem is slightly more complicated. Instead of finding the output value for a numerical input, you must find the output when the input is an algebraic expression:

If $f(z) = z^2 - \dfrac{z}{3}$, what is the value of $f(w + 6)$?

Input the variable expression $(w + 6)$ in place of the independent variable (z) to determine the value of the function:

$$f(w + 6) = (w + 6)^2 - \frac{w + 6}{3}$$

Compare this equation to the equation for $f(z)$. The expression $(w + 6)$ has taken the place of every z in the original equation. In a sense, you are treating the expression $(w + 6)$ as one thing, as if it were a single letter or variable.

The rest is algebraic simplification:

$$f(w + 6) = (w + 6)(w + 6) - \left(\frac{w}{3} + \frac{6}{3} \right)$$

$$= w^2 + 12w + 36 - \frac{w}{3} - 2$$

$$= w^2 + 11\frac{2}{3}w + 34$$

Compound Functions

Imagine putting a number into one magic box, and then putting the output directly into another magic box. This is the situation you have with compound functions:

If $f(x) = x^3 + \sqrt{x}$ and $g(x) = 4x - 3$, what is $f(g(3))$?

The expression $f(g(3))$, pronounced "f of g of 3", looks ugly, but the key to solving compound function problems is to work from the inside out. In this case, start with $g(3)$. Notice that you put the number into g, not into f, which may seem backward at first:

$$g(3) = 4(3) - 3 = 12 - 3 = 9$$

Use the result from the *inner* function g as the new input variable for the *outer* function f:

$$f(g(3)) = f(9) = (9)^3 + \sqrt{9} = 729 + 3 = 732 \qquad \text{The final result is 732.}$$

Note that changing the order of the compound functions changes the answer:

If $f(x) = x^3 + \sqrt{x}$ and $g(x) = 4x - 3$, what is $g(f(3))$?

Again, work from the inside out. This time, start with $f(3)$ (which is now the inner function):

$$f(3) = (3)^3 + \sqrt{3} = 27 + \sqrt{3}$$

Use the result from the *inner* function f as the new input variable for the *outer* function g:

$$g(f(3)) = g(27 + \sqrt{3}) = 4(27 + \sqrt{3}) - 3 = 108 + 4\sqrt{3} - 3 = 105 + 4\sqrt{3}$$

Thus, $g(f(3)) = 105 + 4\sqrt{3}$.

In general, $f(g(x))$ and $g(f(x))$ are **not the same rule overall** and will often lead to different outcomes. As an analogy, think of "putting on socks" and "putting on shoes" as two functions: the order in which you perform these steps obviously matters!

You may be asked to find a value of x for which $f(g(x)) = g(f(x))$. In that case, use variable substitution, working as always from the inside out:

If $f(x) = x^3 + 1$, and $g(x) = 2x$, for what value of x does $f(g(x)) = g(f(x))$?

Simply evaluate as you did in the problems above, using x instead of an input value:

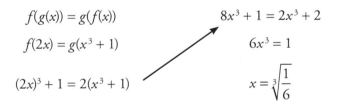

$$f(g(x)) = g(f(x)) \qquad\qquad 8x^3 + 1 = 2x^3 + 2$$
$$f(2x) = g(x^3 + 1) \qquad\qquad 6x^3 = 1$$
$$(2x)^3 + 1 = 2(x^3 + 1) \qquad\qquad x = \sqrt[3]{\frac{1}{6}}$$

Functions with Unknown Constants

On the GRE, you may be given a function with an unknown constant. You will also be given the value of the function for a specific number. You can combine these pieces of information to find the complete function rule:

If $f(x) = ax^2 - x$, and $f(4) = 28$, what is $f(-2)$?

Solve these problems in three steps. First, use the value of the input variable and the corresponding output value of the function to solve for the unknown constant:

$$f(4) = a(4)^2 - 4 = 28$$
$$16a - 4 = 28$$
$$16a = 32$$
$$a = 2$$

MANHATTAN
PREP

Then, rewrite the function, replacing the constant with its numerical value:

$$f(x) = ax^2 - x = 2x^2 - x$$

Finally, solve the function for the new input variable:

$$f(-2) = 2(-2)^2 - (-2) = 8 + 2 = 10$$

Function Graphs

A function can be visualized by graphing it in the coordinate plane. The input variable is considered the **domain** of the function, or the x-coordinate. The corresponding output is considered the **range** of the function, or the y-coordinate.

What is the graph of the function $f(x) = -2x^2 + 1$?

INPUT	OUTPUT	(x, y)
−3	$-2(-3)^2 + 1 = -17$	$(-3, -17)$
−2	$-2(-2)^2 + 1 = -7$	$(-2, -7)$
−1	$-2(-1)^2 + 1 = -1$	$(-1, -1)$
0	$-2(0)^2 + 1 = 1$	$(0, 1)$
1	$-2(1)^2 + 1 = -1$	$(1, -1)$
2	$-2(2)^2 + 1 = -7$	$(2, -7)$
3	$-2(3)^2 + 1 = -17$	$(3, -17)$

Create an **input-output** table by evaluating the function for several input values.

Then, plot points to see the shape of the graph:

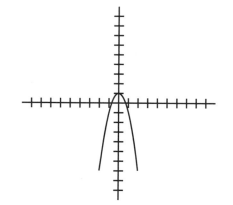

Check Your Skills

10. If $f(x) = \dfrac{1}{x+2} + (x-1)^2$, what is $f(-1)$?

11. If $t(u) = au^2 - 3u + 1$ and $t(3) = 37$, what is a?

12. If $f(x) = 3x - \sqrt{x}$ and $g(x) = x^2$, what is $g(f(4))$?

13. If $g(y) = y^2 - \dfrac{1}{y+1}$, what is $g\left(\dfrac{1}{x}\right)$?

Answers can be found on page 122.

5

Check Your Skills Answer Key

1. **$k = 70$:** Baking time in minutes $= \dfrac{Vk}{T}$

$$30 = \dfrac{150 \times k}{350}$$

$$k = \dfrac{30 \times 350}{150} = 70$$

2. **20:** Deal with the formula in the parentheses first:

$$3\Delta 1 = 3^1 + 1 = 3 + 1 = 4$$
$$-2\Delta(3\Delta 1) = -2\Delta 4$$
$$-2\Delta 4 = (-2)^4 + 4 = 16 + 4 = 20$$

3. **$8\dfrac{1}{8}$:** $2\lambda 16 = \dfrac{16}{2} + \dfrac{2}{16} = 8 + \dfrac{1}{8} = 8\dfrac{1}{8}$

4. **62.5% decrease:**

No numbers are specified, so you should choose values for the original distance and the original rate. Good numbers to pick for the distance are multiples of 2, because the rate is decreased by 1/2. Good numbers to pick for the rate are multiples of 3, because the rate is increased by 1/3:

	Old	New
Distance	12	6
Rate	3	4
Time = Distance/Rate	12/3 = 4	6/4 = 1.5

Percent decrease in time $= \dfrac{\text{change in time}}{\text{original time}} = \dfrac{4 - 1.5}{4} = \dfrac{2.5}{4} = 62.5\%$ decrease.

5. **17:** $S_{11} = 2 \times (11) - 5 = 22 - 5 = 17$

6. **−6:** $B_9 = (-1)^{(9)} \times 9 + 3 = -9 + 3 = -6$

7. **3:** Since you know the value of A_4, you can write the definition for A_4 to solve for A_3, write the definition for A_3 to solve for A_2, and so on:

$$
\begin{aligned}
A_4 &= 2A_3 + 3 & \rightarrow && 45 &= 2A_3 + 3 & \rightarrow && A_3 &= 21 \\
A_3 &= 2A_2 + 3 & \rightarrow && 21 &= 2A_2 + 3 & \rightarrow && A_2 &= 9 \\
A_2 &= 2A_1 + 3 & \rightarrow && 9 &= 2A_1 + 3 & \rightarrow && A_1 &= 3
\end{aligned}
$$

8. **457:** There are $114 - 3 = 111$ "jumps" of 4 between the 3rd and the 114th terms. Since $111 \times 4 = 444$, there is an increase of 444 from the 3rd term to the 114th term: $13 + 444 = 457$.

9. **6:** The units digits of the powers of 7 follow a repeating pattern: **7**, **4**9, **3**43, **2**401, 1680**7**, etc. Pattern = {7, 9, 3, 1}. There are 8 repeats of the pattern from A_1 to A_{32}, inclusive. The pattern begins again on A_{33}, so A_{33} has the same units digit as A_1, which is 7. The units digit of 7^{33} is 7, and $7 - 1 = 6$.

10. **5:** Simply plug in (-1) for each occurrence of x in the function definition and evaluate:

$$f(x) = \frac{1}{x+2} + (x-1)^2 \qquad\qquad f(-1) = \frac{1}{(-1)+2} + ((-1)-1)^2$$

$$f(1) = \frac{1}{1} + (-2)^2 = 1 + 4 = 5$$

11. **5:** Plug in 3 for u in the definition of $t(u)$, set it equal to 37, and solve for a:

$$t(u) = au^2 - 3u + 1 \rightarrow t(3) = a(3)^2 - 3(3) + 1 = 37$$
$$9a - 9 + 1 = 37$$
$$9a = 45$$
$$a = 5$$

12. **100:** First, find the output value of the inner function: $f(4) = 3(4) - \sqrt{4} = 12 - 2 = 10$.

Then, find $g(10)$: $10^2 = 100$.

13. $\dfrac{-x^3 + x + 1}{x^3 + x^2}$: Simply plug in $\left(\dfrac{1}{x}\right)$ for y in $g(y)$, and simplify the expression:

$$g(y) = y^2 - \frac{1}{y+1} \rightarrow g\left(\frac{1}{x}\right) = \left(\frac{1}{x}\right)^2 - \frac{1}{\left(\frac{1}{x}\right)+1}$$

$$g\left(\frac{1}{x}\right) = \frac{1}{x^2} - \frac{1}{\dfrac{x+1}{x}} = \frac{1}{x^2} - \frac{x}{x+1}$$

$$g\left(\frac{1}{x}\right) = \frac{x+1-x^3}{x^2(x+1)} = \frac{-x^3+x+1}{x^3+x^2}$$

Problem Set

1. If $A \lozenge B = 4A - B$, what is the value of $(3 \lozenge 2) \lozenge 3$?

2. If 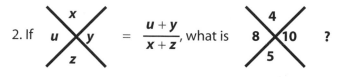 $= \dfrac{u+y}{x+z}$, what is $\quad$?

3. Life expectancy is defined by the formula $\dfrac{2SB}{G}$, where S = shoe size, B = average monthly electric bill in dollars, and G = GRE score. If Melvin's GRE score is twice his monthly electric bill, and his life expectancy is 50, what is his shoe size?

4. The formula for spring factor in a shoe insole is $\dfrac{w^2 + x}{3}$, where w is the width of the insole in centimeters and x is the grade of rubber on a scale of 1 to 9. What is the maximum spring factor for an insole that is 3 centimeters wide?

5. Cost is expressed by the formula tb^4. If b is doubled, by what factor has the cost increased?

    (A) 2   (B) 6   (C) 8   (D) 16   (E) 1/2

6. If the scale model of a cube sculpture is 0.5 cm per every 1 m of the real sculpture, what is the volume of the model, if the volume of the real sculpture is 64 m³?

7. The "competitive edge" of a baseball team is defined by the formula $\sqrt{\dfrac{W}{L}}$, where W represents the number of wins, and L represents the number of losses. This year, the GRE All-Stars had 3 times as many wins and one-half as many losses as they had last year. By what factor did their "competitive edge" increase?

8. If the radius of a circle is tripled, what is the ratio of the area of half the original circle to the area of the whole new circle? (Area of a circle $= \pi r^2$, where r = radius)

For problems #9–10, use the following sequence definition: $A_n = 3 - 8n$.

9. What is A_1?

10. What is $A_{11} - A_9$?

11. A sequence S is defined as follows: $S_n = \dfrac{S_{n+1} + S_{n-1}}{2}$. If $S_1 = 15$ and $S_4 = 10.5$, what is S_2?

12. If $f(x) = 2x^4 - x^2$, what is the value of $f\left(2\sqrt{3}\right)$?

13. If $k(x) = 4x^3 a$, and $k(3) = 27$, what is $k(2)$?

14. If $f(x) = 3x - \sqrt{x}$ and $g(x) = x^2$, what is $f(g(4))$?

15. If $f(x) = 2x^2 - 4$ and $g(x) = 2x$, for what values of x will $f(x) = g(x)$?

16. Which of the following graphs is the graph of function $g(x) = |x - 1| - 1$?

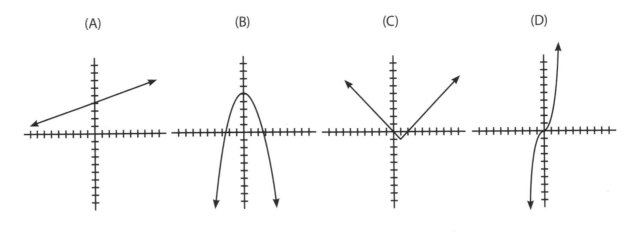

(A)   (B)   (C)   (D)

17. $A_n = 2^n - 1$ for all integers $n \geq 1$

Quantity A   **Quantity B**

The units digit of A_{26} The units digit of A_{34}

18. $P \blacksquare Q = P + 2Q$ for all integers P and Q

Quantity A   **Quantity B**

11 $\blacksquare$ 5   5 $\blacksquare$ 11

19.   The length of a rectangle increased by a factor of 2, and at the same time its area increased by a factor of 6.

Quantity A   **Quantity B**

The factor by which the width of   3
the rectangle increased

Solutions

1. **37:** First, simplify $3 \lozenge 2$: $4(3) - 2 = 12 - 2 = 10$. Then, solve $10 \lozenge 3$: $4(10) - 3 = 40 - 3 = 37$.

2. **2:** Plug the numbers in the grid into the formula, matching up the number in each section with the corresponding variable in the formula: $\dfrac{u + y}{x + z} = \dfrac{8 + 10}{4 + 5} = \dfrac{18}{9} = 2$.

3. **Size 50:**

$$\frac{2SB}{2B} = 50 \qquad \text{Substitute } 2B \text{ for } G \text{ in the formula. Note that the term } 2B \text{ appears}$$
in both the numerator and denominator, so they cancel out.

$$S = 50$$

4. **6:** Determine the maximum spring factor by setting $x = 9$.

Let s = spring factor:

$$s = \frac{w^2 + x}{3} \qquad\qquad s = \frac{(3)^2 + 9}{3} = \frac{18}{3} = 6$$

5. **(D):** Pick numbers to see what happens to the cost when b is doubled. If the original value of b is 2, the cost is $16t$. When b is doubled to 4, the new cost value is $256t$. The cost has increased by a factor of $\dfrac{256}{16}$, or 16.

6. **8 cm³:**

$$V = s^3 \quad \rightarrow \quad 64 = s^3 \quad \rightarrow \quad s = 4 \qquad \text{The length of a side on the real sculpture is 4 m.}$$

$$\frac{0.5 \text{ cm}}{1 \text{ m}} = \frac{x \text{ cm}}{4 \text{ m}} \quad \rightarrow \quad x = 2 \qquad \text{The length of a side on the model is 2 cm.}$$

$$V = s^3 = (2)^3 = 8 \qquad\qquad\qquad\quad \text{The volume of the model is 8.}$$

7. $\sqrt{6}$: Let c = competitive edge:

$$c = \sqrt{\frac{W}{L}}$$

Pick numbers to see what happens to the competitive edge when W is tripled and L is halved. If the original value of W is 2 and the original value of L is 2, the original value of c is $\dfrac{\sqrt{2}}{2} = 1$. If W triples to 6 and L is halved to 1, the new value of c is $\sqrt{\dfrac{6}{1}} = \sqrt{6}$. The competitive edge has increased from 1 to $\sqrt{6}$.

The competitive edge has increased by a factor of $\sqrt{6}$.

8. $\dfrac{1}{18}$: Pick real numbers to solve this problem. Set the radius of the original circle equal to 2. There-fore, the radius of the new circle is equal to 6. Once you compute the areas of both circles, you can find the ratio:

$$\frac{\text{Area of half the original circle}}{\text{Area of the new circle}} = \frac{2\pi}{36\pi} = \frac{1}{18}$$

9. **−5:** $A_n = 3 - 8n$
$$A_1 = 3 - 8(1) = 3 - 8 = -5$$

10. **−16:** $A_n = 3 - 8n$
$$A_{11} = 3 - 8(11) = 3 - 88 = -85$$
$$A_9 = 3 - 8(9) = 3 - 72 = -69$$
$$A_{11} - A_9 = -85 - (-69) = -16$$

11. **13.5:** The easiest way to solve this problem is to write equations for S_2 and S_3 in terms of the other items in the sequence and solve for S_2:

$$S_2 = \frac{S_3 + S_1}{2} \rightarrow S_2 = \frac{S_3 + 15}{2}$$
$$S_3 = \frac{S_4 + S_2}{2} \rightarrow S_3 = \frac{10.5 + S_2}{2}$$

Now substitute the expression for S_3 into the first equation and solve:

$$S_2 = \frac{\left(\dfrac{10.5 + S_2}{2}\right) + 15}{2} \rightarrow 2S_2 = \left(\frac{10.5 + S_2}{2}\right) + 15 \rightarrow 4S_2 = 10.5 + S_2 + 30 \rightarrow 3S_2 = 40.5 \rightarrow S_2 = 13.5$$

By this logic, $S_3 = \dfrac{10.5 + 13.5}{2} = 12$.

12. **276:** $f(x) = 2\left(2\sqrt{3}\right)^4 - \left(2\sqrt{3}\right)^2 = 2(2)^4\left(\sqrt{3}\right)^4 - (2)^2\left(\sqrt{3}\right)^2$
$$= (2 \cdot 16 \cdot 9) - (4 \cdot 3)$$
$$= 288 - 12 = 276$$

13. **8:** $k(3) = 27$. Therefore:

$$4(3)^3 a = 27$$
$$108a = 27$$
$$a = \frac{1}{4} \quad \rightarrow \quad k(x) = 4x^3\left(\frac{1}{4}\right) = x^3 \quad \rightarrow \quad k(2) = (2)^3 = 8$$

14. **44:** First, find the output value of the inner function: $g(4) = 16$. Then, find $f(16)$: $3(16) - \sqrt{16} = 48 - 4 = 44$.

15. $x = \{-1, 2\}$: To find the values for which $f(x) = g(x)$, set the functions equal to each other:

$$2x^2 - 4 = 2x$$
$$2x^2 - 2x - 4 = 0$$
$$2(x^2 - x - 2) = 0$$
$$2(x - 2)(x + 1) = 0$$

$$x - 2 = 0 \qquad\qquad x + 1 = 0$$
$$x = 2 \qquad \text{or} \qquad x = -1$$

16. **(C):** $g(x) = |x - 1| - 1$. This function is an absolute value, which typically has a V-shape. You can identify the correct graph by trying $x = 0$, which yields $g(0) = 0$, the origin. Then, try $x = 1$, which yields $g(1) = -1$ and the point $(1, -1)$. Next, try $x = 2$: $g(2) = |2 - 1| - 1 = 1 - 1 = 0$. These three points fall on the V-shape.

17. **(C):** The powers of 2 have a repeating pattern of four terms for their units digits: $\{2, 4, 8, 6\}$. That means that every fourth term, the pattern repeats. For instance, the 5th term has the same units as the 1st term, because $5 - 1 = 4$. So terms that are four terms apart, or a multiple of 4 terms apart, will have the same units digit.

The 34th term and the 26th term are $34 - 26 = 8$ terms apart. Because 8 is a multiple of 4, the terms will have the same units digit. **The two quantities are equal.** Incidentally, the units digit of A_{26} and A_{34} is 3.

18. **(B):**
$$P \blacksquare Q = P + 2Q \text{ for all}$$
$$\text{integers } P \text{ and } Q$$

Quantity A	**Quantity B**
$11 \blacksquare 5 =$	$5 \blacksquare 11 =$
$(11) + 2 \times (5) =$	$(5) + 2 \times (11) =$
$11 + 10 = \mathbf{21}$	$5 + 22 = \mathbf{27}$

Quantity B is greater.

19. **(C):** Plug in numbers to answer this question. Use a table to organize the information:

	Old	New
Length	2	$2 \times 2 = 4$
Width	1	W
Area	2	$2 \times 6 = 12$

$$4 \times W = 12$$
$$W = 3$$

Compare the new width to the original: $\dfrac{\text{New}}{\text{Old}} = \dfrac{3}{1} = 3$. The width increased by a factor of 3.

The two quantities are equal.

Chapter 6
of
Algebra

Drill Sets

In This Chapter...

Chapter Review: Drill Sets

Chapter Review: Drill Sets

Drill Set 1

Evaluate the following expressions.

1. $19 \times 5 =$
2. $39 - (25 - 17) =$
3. $17(6) + 3(6) =$
4. $3(4 - 2) \div 2 =$
5. $15 \times 3 \div 9 =$
6. $(9 - 5) - (4 - 2) =$
7. $14 - 3(4 - 6) =$
8. $6/3 + 12/3 =$
9. $-5 \times 1 \div 5 =$
10. $\dfrac{-3 + 7}{-4} =$

Evaluate the following expressions.

11. $(4)(-3)(2)(-1) =$
12. $5 - (4 - (3 - (2 - 1))) =$
13. $7 - (6 + 2) =$
14. $7 - (6 - 2) =$
15. $-4(5) - 12/(2 + 4) =$
16. $-3(-2) + 6/3 - (-5) =$
17. $-12 \times 2/(-3) + 5 =$
18. $(6 \times 5) + 14/7 =$
19. $32/(4 + 6 \times 2) =$
20. $-10 - (-3)^2 =$

Evaluate the following expressions.

21. $-5^2 =$
22. $2^3/2 =$
23. $-2^3/2 =$
24. $(3^2 \times 24)/(2^3) =$
25. $36/(2 + 2^2) \times 4 \times (4 + 2) =$
26. $\sqrt{6^2} + (-3^3) =$
27. $5^3 - 5^2 =$
28. $\sqrt{81} - \sqrt{9} =$
29. $[\sqrt{16} + (4 \times 2^3)]/(-2)^2 =$
30. $(3 + (-2)^3)^2 - 3^2 =$

Evaluate the following expressions.

31. $4^3 - 4^2 =$
32. $5^{(2+1)} + 25 =$
33. $(-2)^3 - 5^2 + (-4)^3 =$
34. $(63/3^2)^3/7 =$
35. $5(1) + 5(2) + 5(3) + 5(4) =$
36. $\sqrt{3^4/9} =$
37. $3 \times 7^2 =$
38. $4^2(3 - 1) - 19 + 4(-2) =$
39. $\dfrac{(3+7)(5-3)}{(5 - 4)(5 - 4)} =$
40. $3 \times 99 - 2 \times 99 - 1 \times 99 =$

Drill Set 2

Solve for the variable.

1. $5x - 7 = 28$
2. $14 - 3x = 2$
3. $z - 11 = 1$
4. $3(7 - x) = 4(1.5)$
5. $7x + 13 = 2x - 7$
6. $13 - (-2w) = 6 + 3(11)$
7. $6a/3 = 12 + a$
8. $13x + 2(x + 5) - 7x = -70$
9. $(z - 4)/3 = -12$
10. $y - 15/3 = 7$

Solve for the variable.

11. $y + 3y = 28$
12. $15z + (4z/2) = 51$
13. $3t^3 - 7 = 74$
14. $7(x - 3) + 2 = 16$
15. $z/6 = -8$
16. $1{,}200x + 6{,}000 = 13{,}200$
17. $(1{,}300x + 1{,}700)/43 = 100$
18. $90x + 160 + 5x - 30 + 5x - 30 = 900$
19. $4(x + 2)^3 - 38 = 70$
20. $4(5x + 2) + 44 = 132$

6

Solve for the variable.

21. $\sqrt{x} = 3 \times 5 - 20 \div 4$
22. $-(x)^3 = 64$
23. $x^3 = 8$
24. $4x^3 - 175 = 325$
25. $9 = y^3/3$
26. $-\sqrt{w} = -5$
27. $\dfrac{\sqrt{3x+1}}{2} - 1 = 3$
28. $128 = 2z^3$
29. $5\sqrt[3]{x} + 6 = 51$
30. $\dfrac{\sqrt{x-2}}{5} - 20 = -17$

Isolate x.

31. $3x + 2(x + 2) = 2x + 16$
32. $\dfrac{3x+7}{x} = 10$
33. $4(-3x - 8) = 8(-x + 9)$
34. $3x + 7 - 4x + 8 = 2(-2x - 6)$
35. $2x(4 - 6) = -2x + 12$
36. $\dfrac{3(6-x)}{2x} = -6$
37. $\dfrac{13}{x+13} = 1$
38. $\dfrac{10(3x+4)}{10-5x} = 2$
39. $\dfrac{8-2(-4+10x)}{2-x} = 17$
40. $\dfrac{50(10+3x)}{50+7x} = 50$

Drill Set 3

Solve for the value of both variables in each system of equations. Explanations will follow the four steps discussed in the chapter. Not every step will be necessary to answer every question.

1. $7x - 3y = 5$
   $y = 10$
2. $2h - 4k = 0$
   $k = h - 3$
3. $64 - 2y = x$
   $y = 33$
4. $3q - 2y = 5$
   $y = 2q - 4$
5. $5r - 7s = 10$
   $r + s = 14$
6. $3x + 6y = 69$
   $2x - y = 11$
7. $4w - (5 - z) = 6$
   $w - 3(z + 3) = 10$
8. $6x + 15 - 3y$
   $x + y = 14$
9. $4c + 3t = 33$
   $c + 6 = t + 2$
10. $50x + 20y = 15$
    $10x + 4y = 3$ *(watch out!)*

Practice for Rate problems.

11. $5(t + 1) = d$
    $7t = d + 7$
12. $4t = d$
    $6(t - 1) = d + 4$
13. $50t = d$
    $30t = d - 40$
14. $4r + 10t = 140$
    $r + 25t = 170$
15. $7t = d$
    $5(t - 2) = d - 22$

MANHATTAN
PREP

Many Rates and Distance problems come down to setting up and solving two equations for two variables. Solving these systems of equations is good practice for when you review Rate problems for the GRE.

Practice for other types of word problems.

16. $4x = 3y$
     $x - 2y = -15$
17. $12b = 2g$
     $4g - 3b = 63$
18. $y = 4x + 10$
     $y = 7x - 5$
19. $j + 10 = 2m$
     $j = m - 3$
20. $2s = t$
     $s + t = 36$

Drill Set 4

Distribute the following factored forms (using FOIL).

1. $(x + 2)(x - 3) =$
2. $(2s + 1)(s + 5) =$
3. $(h - 3)(h + 6) =$
4. $(5 + a)(3 + a) =$
5. $(x + y)(x + y) =$

Distribute the following factored forms (using FOIL).

6. $(y + 7)(y + 13) =$
7. $(3 - z)(z + 4) =$
8. $(x + 6)(x - 6) =$
9. $(2x - y)(x + 4y) =$
10. $(x^2 + 5)(x + 2) =$

Factor the following expressions.

11. $18x + 24$
12. $9y - 12y^2$
13. $7x^3 + 84x$
14. $40y + 30x$
15. $5x^4 - 10x^3 + 35x$

Factor the following expressions.

16. $3xy^2 + 6xy$
17. $15a^2b + 30ab - 75ab^2$
18. $2xyz + 6xy - 10yz$
19. $4x^2 + 12x + 8$
20. $2y^3 - 10y^2 + 12y$

Drill Set 5

Solve the following equations. List all possible solutions.

1. $x^2 - 2x = 0$
2. $y^2 + 3y = 0$
3. $z^2 = -5z$
4. $44j - 11jk = 0$
5. $4xy + 2x^2y = 0$

Solve the following equations. List all possible solutions.

6. $y^2 + 4y + 3 = 0$
7. $y^2 - 11y + 30 = 0$
8. $y^2 + 12y + 36 = 0$
9. $c^2 - 23c + 42 = 0$
10. $w^2 + 17w + 60 = 0$

Solve the following equations. List all possible solutions.

11. $a^2 - a - 12 = 0$
12. $x^2 + 8x - 20 = 0$
13. $b^2 - 4b - 32 = 0$
14. $y^2 - 4y - 45 = 0$
15. $x^2 + 9x - 90 = 0$

Solve the following equations. List all possible solutions.

16. $2a^2 + 6a + 4 = 0$
17. $y^2 - 7y + 4 = -6$
18. $x^3 - 3x^2 - 28x = 0$
19. $x^3 - 5x^2 + 4x = 0$
20. $-3x^3 + 6x^2 + 9x = 0$

6

Drill Set Answers

Drill Set 1

1. $19 \times 5 = \mathbf{95}$
Tip: $20 \times 5 = 100$. You have one less five.
$100 - 5 = 95$. Or, use the calculator!

2. $39 - (25 - 17) =$
$39 - 8 = \mathbf{31}$
Tip: You could distribute the minus sign
$(39 - 25 + 17)$ if you prefer, but this method
is less prone to error.

3. $17(6) + 3(6) =$
$102 + 18 = \mathbf{120}$
Tip: If you add 3 sixes to 17 sixes, you will have
20 sixes: $20 \times 6 = 120$. Or, use the calculator!

4. $3 \times (4 - 2) \div 2 =$
$3 \times (2) \div 2 -$
$6 \div 2 = \mathbf{3}$

5. $15 \times 3 \div 9 =$
$45 \div 9 = \mathbf{5}$

6. $(9 - 5) - (4 - 2) =$
$(4) - (2) = \mathbf{2}$

7. $14 - 3(4 - 6) =$
$14 - 3(-2) =$
$14 + 6 = \mathbf{20}$

8. $6/3 + 12/3 =$
$2 + 4 = \mathbf{6}$

9. $-5 \times 1 \div 5 =$
$-5 \div 5 = \mathbf{-1}$

10. $\dfrac{-3+7}{-4} = \dfrac{4}{-4} = \mathbf{-1}$

11. $(4)(-3)(2)(-1) = \mathbf{24}$

Tip: To determine whether a product will be
positive or negative, count the number of positive
and negative terms being multiplied. An even
number of negative terms will give you a positive
product; an odd number of negative terms will
give you a negative product.

12. $5 - (4 - (3 - (2 - 1))) =$
$5 - (4 - (3 - 1)) =$
$5 - (4 - 2) =$
$5 - (2) = \mathbf{3}$
Tip: Start with the inner-most parentheses and
be careful about the signs!

13. $7 - (6 + 2) =$
$7 - (8) = \mathbf{-1}$

14. $7 - (6 - 2) =$
$7 - (4) = \mathbf{3}$

15. $-4(5) - 12/(2 + 4) =$
$-20 - 12/(6) =$
$-20 - 2 = \mathbf{-22}$

16. $-3(-2) + 6/3 - (-5) =$
$6 + 2 + 5 = \mathbf{13}$

17. $-12 \times 2/(-3) + 5 =$
$-24/(-3) + 5 =$
$8 + 5 = \mathbf{13}$

18. $(6 \times 5) + 14/7 =$
$(30) + 2 = \mathbf{32}$

19. $32/(4 + 6 \times 2) =$
$32/(4 + 12) =$
$32/(16) = \mathbf{2}$

20. $-10 - (-3)^2 =$
$-10 - (9) = \mathbf{-19}$
Watch out for the signs!

21. $-5^2 =$

$-5^2 = -25$

Note: Make sure to read this as $-(5^2)$,
NOT: $(-5)^2 = 25$, which would give you 25.

22. $2^3/2 =$

$8/2 = 4$

23. $-2^3/2 =$

$-8/2 = -4$

24. $(3^2 \times 24)/(2^3) =$

$(9 \times 24)/8 = 216/8 = 27$

25. $36/(2 + 2^2) \times 4 \times (4 + 2) =$

$36/(2 + 4) \times 4 \times (6) =$
$36/(6) \times 4 \times 6 =$
$6 \times 4 \times 6 = 144$

26. $\sqrt{6^2} + (-3^3) =$

$6 + (-27) =$
$6 - 27 = -21$

27. $5^3 - 5^2 =$

$125 - 25 = 100$

28. $\sqrt{81} - \sqrt{9} =$

$9 - 3 = 6$

29. $[\sqrt{16} + (4 \times 2^3)] / (-2)^2 =$

$[4 + (4 \times 8)]/4 =$
$[4 + 32]/4 = 36/4 = 9$

30. $(3 + (-2)^3)^2 - 3^2 =$

$(3 - 8)^2 - 9 =$
$(-5)^2 - 9 = 25 - 9 = 16$

31. $4^3 - (4)^2 =$

$64 - 16 = 48$

32. $5^{(2+1)} + 25 =$

$5^3 + 25 = 125 + 25 = 150$

33. $(-2)^3 - 5^2 + (-4)^3 =$

$(-8) - 25 + (-64) =$
$-33 - 64 = -97$

34. $(63/3^2)^3/7$

$(63/9)^3/7 = 7^3/7 = 343/7 = 49$

35. $5(1) + 5(2) + 5(3) + 5(4) =$

$5 + 10 + 15 + 20 = 50$

36. $\sqrt{(3^4/9)} =$

$\sqrt{(81/9)} = \sqrt{9} = 3$

37. $3 \times 7^2 =$

$3 \times 49 =$
147

38. $4^2(3 - 1) - 19 + 4(-2) =$

$4^2(2) - 19 + (-8) =$
$16(2) - 19 - 8 =$
$32 - 27 = 5$

39. $\dfrac{(3+7)(5-3)}{(5-4)(5-4)} = \dfrac{10 \times 2}{1 \times 1} = 20$

40. $3 \times 99 - 2 \times 99 - 1 \times 99 =$

$99(3 - 2 - 1) =$
$99(0) = 0$

Drill Set 2

1. $5x - 7 = 28$

$5x = 35$	Add 7.
$x = 7$	Divide by 5.

2. $14 - 3x = 2$

$-3x = -12$	Subtract 14.
$x = 4$	Divide by -3.

3. $z - 11 = 1$

$z = 12$	Add 11.

4. $3(7 - x) = 4(1.5)$

$21 - 3x = 6$	Simplify
$-3x = -15$	Subtract 21.
$x = 5$	Divide by -3.

MANHATTAN
PREP

5. $7x + 13 = 2x - 7$

    $5x + 13 = -7$ Subtract $2x$.

    $5x = -20$ Subtract 13.

    $x = \mathbf{-4}$ Divide by 5.

6. $13 - (-2w) = 6 + 3(11)$

    $13 + 2w = 6 + 33$ Simplify.

    $2w = 39 - 13$ Subtract 13.

    $2w = 26$ Divide by 2.

    $w = \mathbf{13}$

7. $6a/3 = 12 + a$

    $6a = 3 \times (12 + a)$ Multiply by 3.

    $6a = 36 + 3a$ Simplify.

    $3a = 36$ Subtract $3a$.

    $a = \mathbf{12}$ Divide by 3.

8. $13x + 2(x + 5) - 7x = -70$

    $13x + 2x + 10 - 7x = -70$ Simplify.

    $8x + 10 = -70$ Combine terms.

    $8x = -80$ Subtract 10.

    $x = \mathbf{-10}$ Divide by 8.

9. $(z - 4)/3 = -12$

    $z - 4 = -36$ Multiply by 3.

    $z = \mathbf{-32}$ Add 4.

10. $y - 15/3 = 7$

    $y - 5 = 7$ Simplify.

    $y = \mathbf{12}$ Add 5.

11. $y + 3y = 28$

    $4y = 28$

    $y = \mathbf{7}$

12. $15z + (4z/2) = 51$

    $15z + 2z = 51$

    $17z = 51$

    $z = \mathbf{3}$

13. $3t^3 - 7 = 74$

    $3t^3 = 81$

    $t^3 = 27$

    $t = \mathbf{3}$

14. $7(x - 3) + 2 = 16$

    $7(x - 3) = 14$

    $x - 3 = 2$

    $x = \mathbf{5}$

15. $z/6 = -8$

    $z = \mathbf{-48}$

16. $1{,}200x + 6{,}000 = 13{,}200$

    $1{,}200x = 7{,}200$

    $x = \mathbf{6}$

17. $(1{,}300x + 1{,}700)/43 = 100$

    $1{,}300x + 1{,}700 = 4{,}300$

    $1{,}300x = 2{,}600$

    $x = \mathbf{2}$

18. $90x + 160 + 5x - 30 + 5x - 30 = 900$

    $100x + 100 = 900$

    $100x = 800$

    $x = \mathbf{8}$

19. $4(x + 2)^3 - 38 = 70$

    $4(x + 2)^3 = 108$

    $(x + 2)^3 = 27$

    $x + 2 = 3$

    $x = \mathbf{1}$

20. $4(5x + 2) + 44 = 132$

    $4(5x + 2) = 88$

    $5x + 2 = 22$

    $5x = 20$

    $x = \mathbf{4}$

21. $\sqrt{x} = 3 \times 5 - 20 \div 4$

    $\sqrt{x} = 15 - 5$

    $\sqrt{x} = 10$

    $x = \mathbf{100}$

22. $-(x)^3 = 64$

    $(x)^3 = -64$

    $x = \mathbf{-4}$

6

23. $x^3 = 8$

 $x = \mathbf{2}$

24. $4x^3 - 175 = 325$

 $4x^3 = 500$

 $x^3 = 125$

 $x = \mathbf{5}$

25. $9 = y^3/3$

 $27 = y^3$

 $\mathbf{3} = y$

26. $-\sqrt{w} = -5$

 $\sqrt{w} = 5$

 $w = (5)^2$

 $w = \mathbf{25}$

27. $\dfrac{\sqrt{3x+1}}{2} - 1 = 3$

 $\dfrac{\sqrt{3x+1}}{2} = 4$

 $\sqrt{3x+1} = 8$

 $3x + 1 = 64$

 $3x = 63$

 $x = 21$

28. $128 = 2z^3$

 $64 = z^3$

 $\mathbf{4} = z$

29. $5\sqrt[3]{x} + 6 = 51$

 $5\sqrt[3]{x} = 45$

 $\sqrt[3]{x} = 9$

 $x = 9^3 = \mathbf{729}$

30. $\dfrac{\sqrt{x-2}}{5} - 20 = -17$

 $\dfrac{\sqrt{x-2}}{5} = 3$

 $\sqrt{x-2} = 15$

 $x - 2 = 15^2 = 225$

 $x = \mathbf{227}$

31. $3x + 2(x + 2) = 2x + 16$

 $3x + 2x + 4 = 2x + 16$

 $5x + 4 = 2x + 16$

 $3x + 4 = 16$

 $3x = 12$

 $x = \mathbf{4}$

32. $\dfrac{3x + 7}{x} = 10$

 $3x + 7 = 10x$

 $7 = 7x$

 $\mathbf{1} = x$

33. $4(-3x - 8) = 8(-x + 9)$

 $-12x - 32 = -8x + 72$

 $-32 = 4x + 72$

 $-104 = 4x$

 $\mathbf{-26} = x$

34. $3x + 7 - 4x + 8 = 2(-2x - 6)$

 $-x + 15 = -4x - 12$

 $3x + 15 = -12$

 $3x - -27$

 $x = \mathbf{-9}$

35. $2x(4 - 6) = -2x + 12$

 $2x(-2) = -2x + 12$

 $-4x = -2x + 12$

 $-2x = 12$

 $x = \mathbf{-6}$

36. $\dfrac{3(6 - x)}{2x} = -6$

 $3(6 - x) = -6(2x)$

 $18 - 3x = -12x$

 $18 = -9x$

 $\mathbf{-2} = x$

37. $\dfrac{13}{x + 13} = 1$

 $13 = 1(x + 13)$

 $13 = x + 13$

 $\mathbf{0} = x$

MANHATTAN
PREP

38. $\dfrac{10(3x+4)}{10-5x} = 2$

$10(3x+4) = 2(10-5x)$

$30x + 40 = 20 - 10x$

$40x + 40 = 20$

$40x = -20$

$x = \textbf{-1/2}$

39. $\dfrac{8-2(-4+10x)}{2-x} = 17$

$8 - 2(-4+10x) = 17(2-x)$

$8 + 8 - 20x = 34 - 17x$

$16 - 20x = 34 - 17x$

$16 = 34 + 3x$

$-18 = 3x$

$\textbf{-6} = x$

40. $\dfrac{50(10+3x)}{50+7x} = 50$

$50(10+3x) = 50(50+7x)$

$10 + 3x = 50 + 7x$

$-40 = 4x$

$\textbf{-10} = x$

Drill Set 3

Step 1: Isolate one variable.

Step 2: Substitute for variable.

Step 3: Solve.

Step 4: Substitute solution and solve for other variables

1. Eq. (1): $7x - 3y = 5$

    $7x - 3(10) = 5$

    $7x - 30 = 5$

    $7x = 35$

    $x = 5$

    Answer: $\boldsymbol{x = 5, y = 10}$

    Eq. (2): $y = 10$

    (Step 2) Substitute (10) for y in Eq. (1).

    (Step 3) Solve for x. Simplify grouped terms.

    Add 30.

    Divide by 7.

2. Eq. (1): $2h - 4k = 0$

    $2h - 4(h-3) = 0$

    $2h - 4h + 12 = 0$

    $-2h = -12$

    $h = 6$

    $k = (6) - 3$

    $k = 3$

    Answer: $\boldsymbol{h = 6, k = 3}$

    Eq. (2): $k = h - 3$

    (Step 2) Substitute $(h-3)$ for k in Eq. (1).

    (Step 3) Solve for h. Simplify grouped terms.

    Combine like terms.

    Divide by -2.

    (Step 4) Substitute (6) for h in Eq. (2) and solve for k.

    Simplify.

6

3. Eq. (1): $64 - 2y = x$ Eq. (2): $y = 33$

$64 - 2(33) = x$ (Step 2) Substitute (33) for y in Eq. (1).

$64 - 66 = x$ (Step 3) Solve for x. Simplify.

$-2 = x$

Answer: $\mathbf{y = 33, x = -2}$

4. Eq. (1): $3q - 2y = 5$ Eq. (2): $y = 2q - 4$

$3q - 2(2q - 4) = 5$ (Step 2) Substitute $(2q - 4)$ for y in Eq. (1).

$3q - 4q + 8 = 5$ (Step 3) Solve for q. Simplify grouped terms.

$-q + 8 = 5$ Combine like terms.

$-q = -3$ Subtract 8.

$q = 3$ Divide by -1.

$y = 2(3) - 4$ (Step 4) Substitute (3) for q in Eq. (2). Solve for y.

$y = 6 - 4$ Simplify.

$y = 2$

Answer: $\mathbf{q = 3, y = 2}$

5. Eq. (1): $5r - 7s = 10$ Eq. (2): $r + s = 14$

$r + s = 14$

$r = 14 - s$ (Step 1) Isolate r in Eq. (2). Subtract s.

$5(14 - s) - 7s = 10$ (Step 2) Substitute $(14 - s)$ for r in Eq. (1).

$70 - 5s - 7s = 10$ Simplify grouped terms.

$70 - 12s = 10$ Combine like terms.

$70 = 10 + 12s$ Add 12s.

$60 = 12s$ Subtract 10.

$5 = s$ Divide by 12.

$r + (5) = 14$ (Step 4) Substitute (5) for s in Eq. (2). Solve for r.

$r = 9$ Subtract 5.

Answer: $\mathbf{r = 9, s = 5}$

6. Eq. (1): $3x + 6y = 69$ Eq. (2): $2x - y = 11$

$2x - y = 11$

$-y = -2x + 11$ (Step 1) Isolate y in Eq. (2). Subtract 2x.

$y = 2x - 11$ Divide by -1.

$3x + 6(2x - 11) = 69$ (Step 2) Substitute $(2x - 11)$ for y in Eq. (1).

$3x + 12x - 66 = 69$ (Step 3) Solve for x. Simplify grouped terms.

$15x - 66 = 69$ Combine like terms.

MANHATTAN
PREP

$15x = 135$ | Add 66.
$x = 9$ | Divide by 15.

$2(9) - y = 11$ | (Step 4) Substitute (9) for x in Eq. (2). Solve for y.
$18 - y = 11$ | Simplify.
$18 = 11 + y$ | Add y.
$7 = y$ | Subtract 11.

Answer: $x = 9$, $y = 7$

7. Eq. (1): $4w - (5 - z) = 6$ Eq. (2): $w - 3(z + 3) = 10$

$4w - (5 - z) = 6$ |
$4w - 5 + z = 6$ | Isolate z in Eq. (1). Simplify grouped terms.
$4w + z = 11$ | Add 5.
$z = 11 - 4w$ | Subtract $4w$.

$w - 3(z + 3) = 10$ |
$w - 3z - 9 = 10$ | Simplify Eq. (2). Simplify grouped terms.
$w - 3z = 19$ | Add 9.
$w - 3(11 - 4w) = 19$ | (Step 2) Substitute $(11 - 4w)$ for z in Eq. (2).
$w - 33 + 12w = 19$ | (Step 3) Solve for w. Simplify grouped terms.
$13w \quad 33 = 19$ | Combine like terms.
$13w = 52$ | Add 33.
$w = 4$ | Divide by 13.

$z = 11 - 4w$ |
$z = 11 - 4(4)$ | Substitute (4) for w in the simplified form of Eq. (1).
$z = 11 - 16$ | Simplify.
$z = -5$ | Simplify.

Answer: $w = 4$, $z = -5$

8. Eq. (1): $6x + 15 = 3y$ Eq. (2): $x + y = 14$

$x + y = 14$ |
$x = 14 - y$ | (Step 1) Isolate x in Eq. (2). Subtract y.

$6(14 - y) + 15 = 3y$ | (Step 2) Substitute $(14 - y)$ for x in Eq. (1).
$84 - 6y + 15 = 3y$ | (Step 3) Solve for y. Simplify grouped terms.
$99 - 6y = 3y$ | Combine like terms.
$99 = 9y$ | Add $6y$.
$11 = y$ | Divide by 9.

$x + 11 = 14$ | (Step 4) Substitute (11) for y in Eq (2). Solve for x.
$x = 3$ | Subtract 11.

Answer: $x = 3$, $y = 11$

141

9. Eq. (1):　$4c + 3t = 33$　　　　　　　　Eq. (2):　$c + 6 = t + 2$

$c + 6 = t + 2$
$c + 4 = t$　　　　　　　　　　　　　(Step 1) Isolate t in Eq. (2). Subtract 2.

$4c + 3(c + 4) = 33$　　　　　　　　(Step 2) Substitute $(c + 4)$ for t in Eq. (1).
$4c + 3c + 12 = 33$　　　　　　　　(Step 3) Solve for c. Simplify grouped terms.
$7c + 12 = 33$　　　　　　　　　　Combine like terms.
$7c = 21$　　　　　　　　　　　　　Subtract 12.
$c = 3$　　　　　　　　　　　　　　Divide by 7.

$c + 6 = t + 2$
$(3) + 6 = t + 2$　　　　　　　　　(Step 4) Substitute (3) for c in Eq. (2). Solve for t.
$9 = t + 2$　　　　　　　　　　　　Simplify.
$7 = t$　　　　　　　　　　　　　　Subtract 2.

Answer: **$c = 3$, $t = 7$**

10. Eq. (1):　$50x + 20y = 15$　　　　　　Eq. (2):　$10x + 4y = 3$

$10x + 4y = 3$
$50x + 20y = 15$　　　　　　　　　Multiply Eq. (2) by 5.

***Can't solve**—these are the same equations!*
Tip: You can only solve two equations for two variables if the equations are different.

11. Eq. (1):　$5(t + 1) = d$　　　　　　　Eq. (2):　$7t = d + 7$

$5(t + 1) = d$
$5t + 5 = d$　　　　　　　　　　　(Step 1) Isolate d in Eq. (1). Simplify Eq. (1).

$7t = (5t + 5) + 7$　　　　　　　　(Step 2) Substitute $(5t + 5)$ for d in Eq. (2).
$7t = 5t + 12$　　　　　　　　　　(Step 3) Solve for t. Simplify.
$2t = 12$　　　　　　　　　　　　　Subtract 5t.
$t = 6$　　　　　　　　　　　　　　Divide by 2.

$7(6) = d + 7$　　　　　　　　　　(Step 4) Substitute (6) for t in Eq. (2). Solve for d.
$42 = d + 7$　　　　　　　　　　　Simplify.
$35 = d$　　　　　　　　　　　　　Subtract 7.

Answer: **$t = 6$, $d = 35$**

12. Eq. (1):　$4t = d$　　　　　　　　　　Eq. (2):　$6(t - 1) = d + 4$

$6t - 6 = d + 4$　　　　　　　　　　(Step 1) Simplify grouped terms in Eq. (2).
$6t - 6 = (4t) + 4$　　　　　　　　(Step 2) Substitute $(4t)$ for d in Eq. (2).
$6t = 4t + 10$　　　　　　　　　　(Step 3) Solve for t. Add 6.
$2t = 10$　　　　　　　　　　　　　Subtract 4t.
$t = 5$　　　　　　　　　　　　　　Divide by 2.

6

MANHATTAN
PREP

$4(5) = d$ (Step 4) Substitute (5) for t in Eq. (1). Solve for d.
$20 = d$ Simplify.

Answer : $t = 5$, $d = 20$

13. Eq. (1): $50t = d$ Eq. (2): $30t = d - 40$

$30t = 50t - 40$ (Step 2) Substitute ($50t$) for d in Eq. (2).
$-20t = -40$ (Step 3) Solve for t. Subtract $50t$.
$t = 2$ Divide by -20.
$50(2) = d$ (Step 4) Substitute (2) for t in Eq. (1). Solve for d.
$100 = d$

Answer: $t = 2$, $d = 100$

14. Eq. (1): $4r + 10t = 140$ Eq. (2): $r + 25t = 170$

$r + 25t = 170$
$r = 170 - 25t$ (Step 1) Isolate r in Eq. (2). Subtract $25t$.

$4(170 - 25t) + 10t = 140$ (Step 2) Substitute ($170 - 25t$) for r in Eq. (1).
$680 - 100t + 10t = 140$ (Step 3) Solve for t. Simplify grouped terms.
$680 - 90t = 140$ Combine like terms.
$-90t = -540$ Subtract 680.
$t = 6$ Divide by -90.

$4r + 10(6) = 140$ (Step 4) Substitute (6) for t in Eq. (1). Solve for r.
$4r + 60 = 140$ Simplify.
$4r = 80$ Subtract 60.
$r = 20$ Divide by 4.

Answer: $t = 6$, $r = 20$

15. Eq. (1): $7t = d$ Eq. (2): $5(t - 2) = d - 22$

$5t - 10 = (7t) - 22$ (Step 2) Substitute ($7t$) for d in Eq. (2).
$5t + 12 = 7t$ (Step 3) Solve for t. Add 22.
$12 = 2t$ Subtract $5t$.
$6 = t$ Divide by 2.

$7(6) = d$ (Step 4) Substitute (6) for t in Eq. (1). Solve for d.
$42 = d$ Simplify.

Answer: $t = 6$, $d = 42$

16. Eq. (1): $4x = 3y$ Eq. (2): $x - 2y = -15$

$x - 2y = -15$
$x = -15 + 2y$ (Step 1) Isolate x in Eq. (2). Add $2y$.

6

$4(-15 + 2y) = 3y$ (Step 2) Substitute $(-15 + 2y)$ for x in Eq. (1).
$-60 + 8y = 3y$ (Step 3) Solve for y. Simplify grouped terms.
$-60 = -5y$ Subtract $8y$.
$12 = y$ Divide by -5.

$4x = 3(12)$ (Step 4) Substitute 12 for y in Eq. (1).
$4x = 36$ Simplify.
$x = 9$ Divide by 4.

Answer: $y = 12$, $x = 9$

17. Eq. (1): $12b = 2g$ Eq. (2): $4g - 3b = 63$

$12b = 2g$
$6b = g$ (Step 1) Isolate g in Eq. (1). Divide by 2.

$4(6b) - 3b = 63$ (Step 2) Substitute $(6b)$ for g in Eq. (2).
$24b - 3b = 63$ (Step 3) Solve for b. Simplify.
$21b = 63$ Combine like terms.
$b = 3$ Divide by 21.

$12(3) = 2g$ (Step 4) Substitute (3) for b in Eq. (1). Solve for g.
$36 = 2g$ Simplify.
$g = 18$ Divide by 2.

Answer: $b = 3$, $g = 18$

18. Eq. (1): $y = 4x + 10$ Eq. (2): $y = 7x - 5$

$(4x + 10) = 7x - 5$ (Step 2) Substitute $(4x + 10)$ for y in Eq. (2).
$10 = 3x - 5$ (Step 3) Solve for x. Subtract $4x$.
$15 = 3x$ Add 5.
$5 = x$ Divide by 3.

$y = 4(5) + 10$ (Step 4) Substitute (5) for x in Eq. (1). Solve for y.
$y = 30$ Simplify.

Answer: $x = 5$, $y = 30$

19. Eq. (1): $j + 10 = 2m$ Eq. (2): $j = m - 3$

$(m - 3) + 10 = 2m$ (Step 2) Substitute $(m - 3)$ for j in Eq. (1).
$m + 7 = 2m$ (Step 3) Solve for m. Simplify.
$7 = m$ Subtract m.

$j = (7) - 3$ (Step 4) Substitute (7) for m in Eq. (2). Solve for j.
$j = 4$ Simplify.

Answer: $m = 7$, $j = 4$

MANHATTAN
PREP

20. Eq. (1): $2s = t$ Eq. (2): $s + t = 36$

    $s + (2s) = 36$ (Step 2) Substitute ($2s$) for t in Eq. (2).

    $3s = 36$ (Step 3) Solve for s. Combine like terms.

    $s = 12$ Divide by 3.

    $2(12) = t$ (Step 4) Substitute (12) for s in Eq. (1). Solve for t.

    $24 = t$ Simplify.

    Answer: $s = 12$, $t = 24$

Drill Set 4

1. $(x + 2)(x - 3) = x^2 - 3x + 2x - 6 = \boldsymbol{x^2 - x - 6}$
2. $(2s + 1)(s + 5) = 2s^2 + 10s + s + 5 = \boldsymbol{2s^2 + 11s + 5}$
3. $(h - 3)(h + 6) = h^2 + 6h - 3h - 18 = \boldsymbol{h^2 + 3h - 18}$
4. $(5 + a)(3 + a) = 15 + 5a + 3a + a^2 = \boldsymbol{a^2 + 8a + 15}$
5. $(x + y)(x + y) = x^2 + xy + xy + y^2 = \boldsymbol{x^2 + 2xy + y^2}$
6. $(y + 7)(y + 13) = y^2 + 13y + 7y + 91 = \boldsymbol{y^2 + 20y + 91}$
7. $(3 - z)(z + 4) = 3z + 12 - z^2 - 4z = \boldsymbol{-z^2 - z + 12}$
8. $(x + 6)(x - 6) = x^2 - 6x + 6x - 36 = \boldsymbol{x^2 - 36}$
9. $(2x - y)(x + 4y) = 2x^2 + 8xy - xy - 4y^2 = \boldsymbol{2x^2 + 7xy - 4y^2}$
10. $(x^2 + 5)(x + 2) = \boldsymbol{x^3 + 2x^2 + 5x + 10}$
11. $18x + 24 = \boldsymbol{6(3x + 4)}$
12. $9y - 12y^2 = \boldsymbol{3y(3 - 4y)}$
13. $7x^3 + 84x = \boldsymbol{7x(x^2 + 12)}$
14. $40y + 30x = \boldsymbol{10(4y + 3x)}$
15. $5x^4 - 10x^3 + 35x = \boldsymbol{5x(x^3 - 2x^2 + 7)}$
16. $3xy^2 + 6xy = \boldsymbol{3xy(y + 2)}$
17. $15a^2b + 30ab - 75ab^2 = \boldsymbol{15ab(a + 2 - 5b)}$
18. $2xyz + 6xy - 10yz = \boldsymbol{2y(xz + 3x - 5z)}$
19. $4x^2 + 12x + 8 = 4(x^2 + 3x + 2) = \boldsymbol{4(x + 2)(x + 1)}$
20. $2y^3 - 10y^2 + 12y = 2y(y^2 - 5y + 6) = \boldsymbol{2y(y - 3)(y - 2)}$

Drill Set 5

1. $x^2 - 2x = 0$

    $x(x - 2) = 0$

    $x = 0$

    OR $(x - 2) = 0 \rightarrow x = 2$ Answer: $\boldsymbol{x = 0}$ or $\boldsymbol{2}$

2. $y^2 + 3y = 0$

    $y(y + 3) = 0$

    $y = 0$

    OR $(y + 3) = 0 \rightarrow y = -3$ Answer: $\boldsymbol{y = 0}$ or $\boldsymbol{-3}$

6

3. $z^2 = -5z$

$z^2 + 5z = 0 \rightarrow z(z + 5) = 0$

$z = 0$

OR $(z + 5) = 0 \rightarrow z = -5$ Answer: $z = \mathbf{0}$ or $\mathbf{-5}$

4. $44j - 11jk = 0$

$11j(4 - k) = 0$

$11j = 0 \rightarrow j = 0$

OR $(4 - k) = 0 \rightarrow k = 4$ Answer: $j = \mathbf{0}$ and/or $k = \mathbf{4}$

5. $4xy + 2x^2y = 0$

$2xy(2 + x) = 0$

$2xy = 0 \rightarrow xy = 0 \rightarrow x = 0$ OR $y = 0$

OR $(2 + x) = 0 \rightarrow x = -2$ Answer: $(x = \mathbf{0}$ or $\mathbf{-2})$ and/or $(y = \mathbf{0})$

6. $y^2 + 4y + 3 = 0$

$(y + 1)(y + 3) = 0$

$(y + 1) = 0 \rightarrow y = -1$

$(y + 3) = 0 \rightarrow y = -3$ Answer: $y = \mathbf{-1}$ or $\mathbf{-3}$

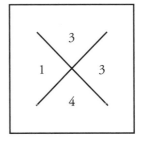

1 & 3 multiply to 3 and sum to 4.

7. $y^2 - 11y + 30 = 0$

$(y - 5)(y - 6) = 0$

$(y - 5) = 0 \rightarrow y = 5$

OR $(y - 6) = 0 \rightarrow y = 6$ Answer: $y = \mathbf{5}$ or $\mathbf{6}$

1 & 30, 2 & 15,
3 & 10, and 5 & 6 multiply to 30. 5
& 6 sum to 11.

8. $y^2 + 12y + 36 = 0$
    $(y + 6)(y + 6) = 0$
    $(y + 6) = 0 \rightarrow y = -6$
    OR $(y + 6) = 0 \rightarrow y = -6$

Answer: $y = -6$
(same result either way)

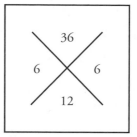

1 & 36, 2 & 18,
3 & 12, 4 & 9, and
6 & 6 multiply to 36. 6 & 6 sum to 12.

9. $c^2 - 23c + 42 = 0$
    $(c - 21)(c - 2) = 0$
    $(c - 21) = 0 \rightarrow c = 21$
    OR $(c - 2) = 0 \rightarrow c = 2$

Answer: $c = 21$ or 2

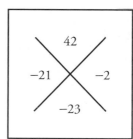

1 & 42, 2 & 21,
3 & 14, and 6 & 7 multiply to 42.
2 & 21 sum to 23.

10. $w^2 + 17w + 60 = 0$
    $(w + 12)(w + 5) = 0$
    $(w + 12) = 0 \rightarrow w = -12$
    OR $(w + 5) = 0 \rightarrow w = -5$

Answer: $w = -12$ or -5

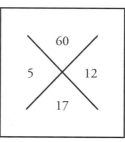

1 & 60, 2 & 30,
3 & 20, 4 & 15,
5 & 12, and 6 & 10 multiply to 60.
5 & 12 sum to 17.

11. $a^2 - a - 12 = 0$
    $(a - 4)(a + 3) = 0$
    $(a - 4) = 0 \rightarrow a = 4$
    OR $(a + 3) = 0 \rightarrow a = -3$

Answer: $a = 4$ or -3

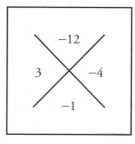

1 & 12, 2 & 6 and
3 & 4 multiply to 12. The
difference of 3 & 4 is 1.

6

12. $x^2 + 8x - 20 = 0$

$(x + 10)(x - 2) = 0$

$(x + 10) = 0 \rightarrow x = -10$

OR $(x - 2) = 0 \rightarrow x = 2$ Answer: $x = \boldsymbol{-10}$ or $\boldsymbol{2}$

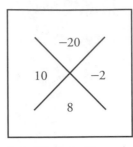

1 & 20, 2 & 10, and
4 & 5 multiply to 20. The difference
of 2 & 10 is 8.

13. $b^2 - 4b - 32 = 0$

$(b - 8)(b + 4) = 0$

$(b - 8) = 0 \rightarrow b = 8$

OR $(b + 4) = 0 \rightarrow b = -4$ Answer: $b = \boldsymbol{8}$ or $\boldsymbol{-4}$

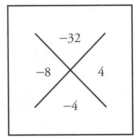

1 & 32, 2 & 16, and
4 & 8 multiply to 32. The difference
of 4 & 8 is 4.

14. $y^2 - 4y - 45 = 0$

$(y - 9)(y + 5) = 0$

$(y - 9) = 0 \rightarrow y = 9$

OR $(y + 5) = 0 \rightarrow y = -5$ Answer: $y = \boldsymbol{9}$ or $\boldsymbol{-5}$

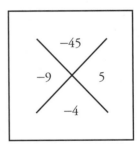

1 & 45, 3 & 15, and 5 & 9
multiply to 45. The difference
of 5 & 9 is 4.

15. $x^2 + 9x - 90 = 0$

$(x + 15)(x - 6) = 0$

$(x + 15) = 0 \rightarrow x = -15$

OR $(x - 6) = 0 \rightarrow x = 6$ Answer: $x = \boldsymbol{-15}$ or $\boldsymbol{6}$

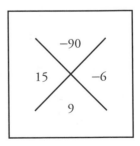

1 & 90, 2 & 45,
3 & 30, 5 & 18,
6 & 15, and 9 & 10 multiply to 90.
The difference of 6 & 15 is 9.

16. $2a^2 + 6a + 4 = 0$

    $2(a^2 + 3a + 2) = 0 \rightarrow 2(a + 2)(a + 1) = 0$

    $(a + 2) = 0 \rightarrow a = -2$

    OR $(a + 1) = 0 \rightarrow a = -1$ Answer: $a = $ **−2** or **−1**

17. $y^2 - 7y + 4 = -6$

    $y^2 - 7y + 10 = 0 \rightarrow (y - 2)(y - 5) = 0$

    $(y - 2) = 0 \rightarrow y = 2$

    OR $(y - 5) = 0 \rightarrow y = 5$ Answer: $y = $ **2** or **5**

18. $x^3 - 3x^2 - 28x = 0$

    $x(x^2 - 3x - 28) = 0 \rightarrow x(x - 7)(x + 4) = 0$

    $x = 0$

    OR $(x - 7) = 0 \rightarrow x = 7$

    OR $(x + 4) = 0 \rightarrow x = -4$ Answer: $x = $ **0** or **7** or **−4**

19. $x^3 - 5x^2 + 4x = 0$

    $x(x^2 - 5x + 4) = 0 \rightarrow x(x - 1)(x - 4) = 0$

    $x = 0$

    OR $(x - 1) = 0 \rightarrow x = 1$

    OR $(x - 4) = 0 \rightarrow x = 4$ Answer: $x = $ **0** or **1** or **4**

20. $-3x^3 + 6x^2 + 9x = 0$

    $-3x(x^2 - 2x - 3) = 0 \rightarrow -3x(x - 3)(x + 1) = 0$

    $-3x = 0 \rightarrow x = 0$

    OR $(x - 3) = 0 \rightarrow x = 3$

    OR $(x + 1) = 0 \rightarrow x = -1$ Answer: $x = $ **0** or **3** or **−1**

6

Chapter 7 of Algebra

Algebra Practice Question Sets

In This Chapter...

Easy Practice Question Set

1. a, b, c are integers, such that $a < b < c$.

Quantity A	**Quantity B**
ac	bc

2.
$$\frac{x-1}{x} = 2$$

Quantity A	**Quantity B**
x	-1

3. If $r = 2s$ and $t = 3r$, what is s in terms of t?

    (A) $\dfrac{t}{6}$

    (B) $\dfrac{t}{3}$

    (C) $\dfrac{2t}{3}$

    (D) $\dfrac{3t}{2}$

    (E) $6t$

4. If $a + b = 2$ and $3a - b = -14$, then what is ab?

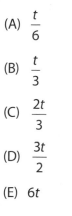

5. Which of the following is a solution of $x^2 + 2x - 8 = 7$?

    (A) 4
    (B) −3
    (C) 2
    (D) 3
    (E) 5

6.
$$x < 0$$

Quantity A	**Quantity B**
$|x|$	$-x$

7

7. A sequence $a_1, a_2, \ldots$ is defined such that each term is 3 less than the preceding term. Which of the following equations is consistent with this definition?

(A) $a_{n+1} - 3 = a_n$

(B) $a_{n+1} + 3 = a_n$

(C) $3 - a_n = a_{n+1}$

(D) $3 - a_{n+1} = a_n$

(E) $a_n + 3 = a_{n+1}$

8. $t > 1$

Quantity A   **Quantity B**

$$\frac{2t+5}{3}$$ $3t$

9.

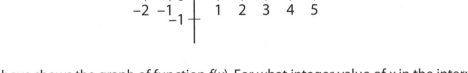

The plot above shows the graph of function $f(x)$. For what integer value of x in the interval shown does $f(x) = x + 1$?

10. At a graduation, guests sit in rows such that there are p people in the first row, $p + 1$ people sit in the second row, $p + 2$ people sit in the third row, and so on. How many more people sit in row n than in the second row?

(A) $n + 2$

(B) $n + 1$

(C) n

(D) $n - 1$

(E) $n - 2$

MANHATTAN
PREP

11. $\langle\!\!\langle n \rangle\!\!\rangle = \left(\dfrac{1}{n}\right)^n$ for all integers $n > 0$. What is the value of $\langle\!\!\langle 3 \rangle\!\!\rangle$?

    (A) $\dfrac{1}{27}$

    (B) $\dfrac{1}{3}$

    (C)   1

    (D)   3

    (E)   27

12. $a \circ b = \dfrac{ab}{a+b}$ for all a, b that satisfy $a \neq -b$. What is the value of $(-4) \circ 2$?

    (A) -4

    (B) -2

    (C) $-\dfrac{4}{3}$

    (D) $\dfrac{4}{3}$

    (E)   4

13. The flavor intensity F of a sauce is given by the formula $F = \dfrac{P^3 S}{A^2}$, where P is piquancy, S is sweetness, and A is acidity. What is the flavor intensity of a sauce with piquancy of 2, sweetness of 1.2, and acidity of 0.4?

    □

14. $$c < -1$$

Quantity A	**Quantity B**
$6c - 3$	$3c - 5$

15. If $8x - 14 - 2y = -10x$ and $3x + 7y - 3 = 5y + 4$, what is the value of $x - y$?

    (A) -1

    (B)   0

    (C)   1

    (D)   2

    (E)   3

16. The distance between q and -1 on the number line equals 5.

Quantity A	Quantity B
$|q|$	3

17.
$$(3x + 1)(2x - 2) = 6x^2 - 10$$

Quantity A	Quantity B
x	2

18.
$$r + s + t > 1 \text{ and } 0 > s + t$$

Quantity A	Quantity B
1	r

19.
$$f(x) = 3x + 1 \text{ and } g(x) = x^2 - 3$$

Quantity A	Quantity B
$f(4)$	$g(4)$

20. If $p + q = 3$ and $p - q = 17$, then $pq =$

┌─────────┐
│   │
└─────────┘

7

Easy Practice Question Solutions

1. **(D):** If all three numbers are positive, bc will be greater, because $b > a$. However, if all three numbers are negative, then ac will be greater. For example, if $a = -5$, $b = -4$, and $c = -3$, then $ac = 15$ and $bc = 12$. Therefore, **the relationship cannot be determined**.

2. **(C):** Solve the equation for x by first multiplying both sides by x in order to clear the fraction: $x - 1 = 2x$. Next, collect all x terms on one side: $-1 = 2x - x = x$. Therefore, $x = -1$ and **the two quantities are equal**.

3. **(A):** You can solve this problem in two ways. One is to use algebra. You want to relate s to t, when you have equations relating each of them to r. The problem is that one equation involves r and the other involves $3r$. You can get around this by multiplying the first equation by 3 on both sides, so as to obtain $3r$: $(3) \times r = (3) \times 2s$, so $3r = 6s$. From the second equation, you know that $3r = t$. Therefore, $3r = 6s = t$, so $s = \dfrac{t}{6}$.

The other option is to pick numbers. Suppose you set $s = 2$. Then, from the first equation, $r = 4$, and from the second equation, $t = 3 \times 4 = 12$, so $s = \dfrac{t}{6}$.

4. **−15:** You are given a system of two equations with two variables. Probably the simplest solution method in this case is to add the equations together, because $+b$ and $-b$ will cancel when you do so:

$$\begin{array}{r} a + b = 2 \\ +\quad 3a - b = -14 \\ \hline 4a \qquad = -12 \end{array}$$

Therefore, $a = -3$. You can then substitute this value into the first equation to obtain $b = 5$. Multiplication yields $ab = (-3)(5) = -15$.

5. **(D):** In order to solve a quadratic equation, you must bring all terms to one side and factor:

$$x^2 + 2x - 15 = 0$$
$$(x + 5)(x - 3) = 0$$

The two solutions for x are -5 and 3. Only the latter appears in the answer choices.

6. **(C):** The absolute value of a quantity is the quantity itself (if it is greater than or equal to 0) or the negative of the quantity (if the original quantity is less than or equal to 0). In this case, because you are told that x is negative, the absolute value of x is $-x$. For instance, if $x = -3$, then $|x| = -(-3) = 3$.

7. **(B):** If each term in the sequence is 3 less than the preceding term, you can express the relationship as $a_{n+1} = a_n - 3$. Adding 3 to both sides results in $a_{n+1} + 3 = a_n$. Alternatively, you could pick representative numbers. Suppose $a_n = 5$ and $a_{n+1} = 2$. You can determine that choice (B) is correct by substituting these values into the five answer choices—all the choices except choice (B) fail.

8. **(B):** First, multiply both sides by 3 to clear the fraction. Multipying by a positive number does not affect the comparison:

$$2t + 5 \qquad\qquad\qquad\qquad\qquad\qquad 9t$$

Now, subtract $2t$ from both columns (again, not affecting the comparison):

$$5 \qquad\qquad\qquad\qquad\qquad\qquad 7t$$

Because $t > 1$, $7t$ is greater than 5. Therefore, **Quantity B is greater.**

9. **−1:** You can solve this problem by inspection of the graph. For more detail and verification, values of the function are tabulated below:

x	$x + 1$	$f(x)$
−2	−1	1
−1	**0**	**0**
0	1	2
1	2	5
2	3	4
3	4	3
4	5	3
5	6	4

It is clear that the only integer value of x for which $f(x) = x + 1$ is $x = -1$.

10. **(E):** You can calculate the data to better observe the pattern:

Row	Number of people
1	p
2	$p + 1$
3	$p + 2$
...	...
n	$p + (n - 1)$

The desired difference is found by $p + (n - 1) - (p + 1) = n - 1 - 1 = n - 2$. Another, perhaps more elegant, method is to observe that the difference in the number of people seated in any two rows is equal to the difference in the row numbers themselves. For example, there is 1 more person seated in row 2 versus row 1 $(2 - 1 = 1)$, 2 more people seated in row 3 versus row 1 $(3 - 1 = 2)$, and so on. Therefore, there will be $n - 2$ more people seated in row n than in row 2.

11. **(A):** $\langle 3 \rangle = \left(\dfrac{1}{3}\right)^3 = \dfrac{1}{3^3} = \dfrac{1}{27}$

12. **(E):** $(-4) \cdot 2 = \dfrac{(-4) \times 2}{-4+2} = \dfrac{-8}{-2} = 4$. Note that this is *not* the same as $-(4 \circ 2)$.

13. **60:** Plug the given values into the formula and evaluate: $F = \dfrac{2^3 \times 1.2}{(0.4)^2} = \dfrac{8 \times 1.2}{0.16} = \dfrac{9.6}{0.16} = 60$. If you

use the calculator in this problem, you must be careful to use parentheses around $(0.4)^2$ in the denominator, because otherwise the operations "$\div 0.4 \times 0.4$" would cancel each other out.

14. **(B):** You should manipulate the quantities so that the c terms are together and the constant terms are together. This can be done by subtracting $3c$ from both quantities, and adding 3 to both quantities:

$$
\begin{array}{cc}
6c - 3 & 3c - 5 \\
-3c + 3 & -3c + 3 \\
\hline
3c & -2
\end{array}
$$

Next, divide both sides by 3 to isolate c:

$$
\begin{array}{cc}
c & \dfrac{-2}{3}
\end{array}
$$

Since the problem explicitly states that $c < -1$, you know that Quantity A will always be more negative than Quantity B. Thus, **Quantity B is greater**.

15. **(A):** You should add/subtract terms to move the x and y terms to the left-hand side of the equation and the constant terms to the right-hand side of the equation:

$$
\begin{array}{lll}
8x - 14 - 2y = -10x & \rightarrow & 18x - 2y = 14 \\
3x + 7y - 3 = 5y + 4 & \rightarrow & 3x + 2y = 7
\end{array}
$$

Next, eliminate the y terms by adding the two equations together:

$$
\begin{array}{r}
18x - 2y = 14 \\
+\ \ 3x + 2y = \ 7 \\
\hline
21x \quad\ \ = 21
\end{array}
$$

Therefore, $x = 1$, and you can plug this back into the second equation to find $y = 2$. Therefore, $x - y = -1$ and **choice (A) is correct**.

16. **(A):** Since q is 5 units away from -1 on the number line, $q = 4$ or -6.

This gives values for $|q|$ of either 4 or 6, both of which are greater than 3. Therefore, **Quantity A is greater**.

17. **(C):** You can use FOIL to distribute the left-hand side of the given equation:

$$(3x + 1)(2x - 2) = 6x^2 - 10$$
$$6x^2 - 6x + 2x - 2 = 6x^2 - 10$$

Eliminating the $6x^2$ terms from each side:

$$-6x + 2x - 2 = -10$$
$$-4x = -8$$
$$x = 2$$

Thus, **the two quantities are equal**.

18. **(B):** The given information tells you that $r + s + t > 1$ and that the sum of s and t is negative. You can reason thusly: in order for the left-hand side of that first inequality $(r + s + t)$ to be greater than 1 given that $(s + t)$ is negative, r will certainly have to be greater than 1. If, for example, $(s + t) = -1$, then r will have to be greater than 2. If, for example, $(s + t) = -5$, then r will have to be greater than 6. If $(s + t)$ is just barely less than 0, then r will have to be *at least* just barely greater than 1. Therefore, r will always be greater than 1.

Alternatively, you could simply line up the two inequalities—the signs must face the same direction—and add them together:

$$r + s + t > 1$$
$$+ \quad\quad 0 > \quad s + t$$
$$\overline{r + s + t > 1 + s + t}$$

Since $(s + t)$ appears on both sides of the inequality, you can subtract $(s + t)$ from both sides to arrive at $r > 1$. Thus, **Quantity B is greater**.

19. **(C):** $f(4) = 3(4) + 1 = 13$ and $g(4) = 4^2 - 3 = 13$. Therefore, **the two quantities are equal**.

20. **−70:** Because the q terms have equal coefficients of opposite signs in the two equations, you can add the equations together to solve for p quickly—the q terms will drop out when the equations are added together:

$$p + q = \quad 3$$
$$+ \quad p - q = 17$$
$$\overline{2p \quad\quad = 20}$$

Thus, $p = 10$. Plugging this back into the first equation, you get $(10) + q = 3$, so $q = -7$, and thus $pq = (10)(-7) = -70$.

Medium Practice Question Set

1. x and y are positive integers and $x > y$.

Quantity A	**Quantity B**
$x^2 - y^2$	$x + y$

2.

Quantity A	**Quantity B**
$\left(\sqrt{x} + \sqrt{y}\right)\left(\sqrt{x} - \sqrt{y}\right)$	$x - y$

3.
$$5a + 3b = 2(a - b)$$
$$6a + 4b = 12$$

Quantity A	**Quantity B**
b	-5

4.
$$xy < 0 \text{ and } \frac{a}{x} > \frac{b}{y}$$

Quantity A	**Quantity B**
ay	bx

5. Consider the function $f(x) = x^2 - 5x$. For which value(s) of x does $f(x) = 14$?

Indicate __all__ that apply.

- A   19
- B   14
- C   7
- D   2
- E   0
- F   −2
- G   −7

6.

$$\left(\frac{p}{q}\right)^2 = 4$$

Quantity A	**Quantity B**
p	$2q$

7. If $\dfrac{x+2y}{2x-y} = 2$, then $x =$

    (A) 0

    (B) $\dfrac{4y}{5}$

    (C) y

    (D) $\dfrac{4y}{3}$

    (E) $3y$

8. $(x + y)^2 - (x^2 - y^2) =$

    (A) $(x - y)^2$
    (B) $2y^2$
    (C) $2xy$
    (D) $2x(y - x)$
    (E) $2y(x + y)$

9. A function is defined by $f(x) = x^2 + 4x - 5$. What is the minimum value of $f(x)$?

    (A)   1
    (B)   0
    (C) −5
    (D) −8
    (E) −9

10.

$$x + y < 0$$
$$y - x > 0$$

Quantity A	**Quantity B**
y	0

11. If the product of $\dfrac{ab}{c}$ and $\dfrac{b}{cd}$ is negative, which two of the following variables must have a product that is less than zero?

    Indicate <u>two</u> such variables.

    [A] a
    [B] b
    [C] c
    [D] d

12. If the total weight of the pumpkins in a pumpkin patch increases by a factor of 10 while the number of pumpkins decreases by 20%, by what factor does the average weight of a pumpkin in the pumpkin patch increase?

    (A) 2
    (B) 8
    (C) 9.8
    (D) 12
    (E) 12.5

13. If $3c + 2d = 8$ and $c < -1$, which one of the following could be a value for d?

    (A) 2.5
    (B) 3.5
    (C) 4.5
    (D) 5.5
    (E) 6.5

14. Assume the function $f(x)$ is defined as follows: $f(x) = (x - 4)^2 + \sqrt{x+3} + \dfrac{5}{x+2}$. For which of the following values of x is $f(x)$ defined?

    Indicate <u>all</u> such values.

    [A] -5
    [B] -4
    [C] -3
    [D] -2
    [E] -1

7

15. In a sequence $a_1, a_2, \ldots$, each term is defined as $a_n = \dfrac{1}{2^n}$. Which of the following expressions represents the sum of the first 10 terms of a_n?

(A) $1 - \dfrac{1}{2^{10}}$

(B) $1 - \dfrac{1}{2^9}$

(C) $1 + \dfrac{1}{2^9}$

(D) $1 + \dfrac{1}{2^{10}}$

(E) $1 + \dfrac{1}{2^{11}}$

16. Set A is the set of all integers x satisfying the inequality $4 < |x| < 9$.

Quantity A

The absolute value of the smallest integer in Set A

Quantity B

The number of integers in Set A

17. x and y are both positive integers.

Quantity A

$|x + y|$

Quantity B

$|x| - |y|$

18. If the average of x and y equals 40, the average of y and z equals 60, and the average of x, y, and z equals 30, then the average of x and z equals what?

19. A customer purchases pickles and onions from a local produce store. If an onion costs 3 times as much as a pickle, which <u>two</u> of the following sets of purchases would have the same cost?

Indicate the <u>two</u> choices that apply.

[A] 9 onions and 3 pickles
[B] 7 onions and 5 pickles
[C] 7 onions and 9 pickles
[D] 5 onions and 12 pickles
[E] 5 onions and 14 pickles

20. $x^2 - 10x + 13 = k$. If one of the solutions to the equation is $x = 4$, what is the other solution for x?

Medium Practice Question Solutions

1. **(D):** It is helpful to recognize that $x^2 - y^2$ factors into $(x + y)(x - y)$. Divide both Quantities by $(x + y)$ to cancel that common positive factor. Now compare $x - y$ to 1. Since $x > y$, $x - y$ must be positive. Thus, Quantity A will usually be greater than 1. However, $x - y$ could equal 1, in which case the Quantities will be equal. Therefore, **the relationship cannot be determined**.

2. **(C):** The efficient approach to this problem is to recognize that this is a variant of the *difference of squares* special product: $(a + b)(a - b) = a^2 - b^2$. The distinction is that each of the exponents in this expression is halved (remember, $x^{1/2} = \sqrt{x}$). Thus, **the two quantities are equal**.

Otherwise, the problem can be solved by distributing the expression in Quantity A to get:

$$\left(\sqrt{x} + \sqrt{y}\right)\left(\sqrt{x} - \sqrt{y}\right) = x - \sqrt{xy} + \sqrt{xy} - y = x - y$$

Alternatively, you can pick numbers. For example, if you pick $x = 25$ and $y = 4$, you get:

$$\left(\sqrt{25} + \sqrt{4}\right)\left(\sqrt{25} - \sqrt{4}\right) = (5 + 2)(5 - 2) = (7)(3) = 21, \text{ and } 25 - 4 = 21$$

3. **(A):** The easiest way to determine a value for b is to manipulate and combine the equations to eliminate a. To begin with, simplify the first equation by distributing the 2 and combining like terms:

$$5a + 3b = 2(a - b)$$
$$5a + 3b = 2a - 2b$$
$$3a + 5b = 0$$

Since you want the a terms in the two equations to cancel out, multiply this equation through by -2:

$$-6a - 10b = 0$$

It is now possible to add the two equations and cancel out the a terms:

$$
\begin{array}{r}
6a + 4b = 12 \\
+ \quad -6a - 10b = 0 \\
\hline
-6b = 12 \\
-b = 2
\end{array}
$$

Therefore, **Quantity A is greater**.

Alternatively, you could have solved for a in one equation, plugged this expression into the second equation, and solved for b.

4. **(B):** Since xy is less than 0, x and y must have opposite signs. Because you know one of them is negative, when you simplify the second expression (by multiplying through by xy), you must flip the inequality sign, yielding:

$$(xy)\frac{a}{x} > \frac{b}{y}(xy) \ \rightarrow \ ay < bx$$

Therefore, **Quantity B is greater**.

5. **(C) and (F):** Setting the value of $f(x) = 14$ in the original function gives the quadratic equation $x^2 - 5x = 14$. Subtract 14 from both sides to get $x^2 - 5x - 14 = 0$. You now need to find two real numbers such that the product of the numbers is -14 and the sum is -5. The numbers you are looking for are -7 and 2 (2 and 7 are the only prime factors of 14, which makes this a fairly easy search). You can therefore rewrite the equation as $(x - 7)(x + 2) = 0$, resulting in a solution set for x of $= \{-2,7\}$.

Alternatively, you could try plugging each of the answer choices into the function to determine which x values result in a function value of 14. Only choices (C) and (F) accomplish this.

6. **(D):** The square of $\frac{p}{q}$ equals 4, so $\frac{p}{q}$ must equal either 2 or -2. In the former case, $p = 2q$, while in the latter case, $p = -2q$. Therefore, **it cannot be determined which quantity is greater**. Note that you might reach the wrong answer if you were to work backwards from the comparison to the equation, by assuming that the two quantities are equal: $p = 2q$ certainly satisfies the given equation, but it is not the only solution.

7. **(D):** First, eliminate the fraction by multiplying both sides by $2x - y$:

$$x + 2y = 2(2x - y) = 4x - 2y$$

Next, collect x terms on one side and y terms on the other:

$$2y + 2y = 4x - x, \text{ or } 4y = 3x$$

Finally, divide by 3 to solve for x:

$$x = \frac{4y}{3}$$

8. **(E):** Expand the first term and subtract: $(x + y)^2 - (x^2 - y^2) = x^2 + 2xy + y^2 - x^2 + y^2 = 2y^2 + 2xy = 2y(x + y)$. Note that, when $(x^2 - y^2)$ is subtracted, the leading minus sign applies to both terms, turning the $-y^2$ into $-(-y^2) = y^2$.

Alternatively, you could pick numbers. Suppose that $x = 3$ and $y = 2$. In that case, $(x + y)^2 = 5^2 = 25$ and $x^2 - y^2 = 9 - 4 = 5$, so that the final result is $25 - 5 = 20$. Only choice (E) gives this result when you substitute your values for x and y.

MANHATTAN
PREP

9. **(E):** You can factor this quadratic as follows: $x^2 + 4x - 5 = (x - 1)(x + 5)$. This means that the solutions for $f(x) = 0$ are $x = 1$ and $x = -5$. A quadratic reaches its extreme value halfway between these solutions—that is, when $x = \dfrac{1 + (-5)}{2} = -2$. Thus, the extreme value is $f(-2) = 4 + 4(-2) - 5 = -9$.

Alternatively, you could make a table of values for x and $f(x)$:

x	-5	-4	-3	-2	-1	0	1
$f(x)$	0	-5	-8	-9	-8	-5	0

Of course, the challenge with tabulating values is that you do not know ahead of time what values to try, so the amount of effort involved could be substantial—with plenty of room for mathematical error.

10. **(D):** The most effective way to combine two inequalities is to line up the inequality symbols and add both sides. However, this can only be done if the inequality symbols face in the same direction. That is not the case here. Therefore, the first step is to "flip" one of the inequalities. You can do so by multiplying both sides of the second inequality by -1, for example:

$$x + y < 0$$
$$x - y < 0$$

At this point, you can add the inequalities, resulting in $2x < 0$ or, dividing by 2, $x < 0$. You know from the original form of the second inequality (by subtracting x from both sides of the inequality) that y is greater than x. However, you still do not know whether y is greater than or less than 0.

11. **(A)** and **(D):** You are given the following relationship: $\left(\dfrac{ab}{c}\right)\left(\dfrac{b}{cd}\right) < 0$. Multiplying out gives $\dfrac{ab^2}{c^2 d} < 0$. Because they are squares, b^2 and c^2 must be positive, so you can divide through by those expressions to obtain $\dfrac{a}{d} < 0$. This can only be true when a and d have opposite signs. In that case, their product will be negative as well.

12. **(E):** The simplest way to solve a problem such as this (a formula problem with unspecified amounts) is to make the math concrete by picking suitable numbers. Suppose that initially there were 10 pumpkins in the patch, with a total weight of 20 pounds. The average weight of a pumpkin in the patch was therefore $\dfrac{20}{10} = 2$ pounds. Afterwards, the total weight of the pumpkins increased to $20 \times 10 = 200$ pounds, while the number of pumpkins decreased to $10 - \dfrac{20}{100} \times 10 = 8$. The new average weight of a pumpkin in the patch is $\dfrac{200}{8} = 25$ pounds. The average weight has increased by a factor of $\dfrac{25}{2} = 12.5$.

13. **(E):** The first step is to solve for d in terms of c:

$$3c + 2d = 8$$
$$2d = 8 - 3c$$
$$d = \frac{8 - 3c}{2} = 4 - 1.5c$$

Given that $c < -1$, you can use extreme values to solve for d by setting c equal to LT(−1):

$$d = 4 - 1.5c = 4 - 1.5 \times \text{LT}(-1) = 4 + \text{GT}(1.5) = \text{GT}(5.5)$$

Thus, d must be *greater than* 5.5, and only choice (E) fits this description. Note the switch from LT to GT: subtracting a "less than" extreme value is the same as adding a "greater than" extreme value.

14. **(C) and (E):** Because $f(x)$ includes the term $\sqrt{x + 3}$, x cannot be less than −3, because the square root of a negative number is not a real number. This eliminates choices (A) and (B). Furthermore, because $f(x)$ includes the term $\frac{5}{x + 2}$, x cannot equal −2, because any fraction with 0 in the denominator is either undefined or indeterminate. Therefore, choice (D) is eliminated. Only choices (C) and (E) remain.

Note that the first term in the function, $(x - 4)^2$, does not affect the range of potential values for x. That term is defined for any value of x.

15. **(A):** Calculate the first few terms of the sequence using the definition $a_n = \frac{1}{2^n}$ and keep a running total of the sum:

n	a_n	Sum of a_1 through a_n
1	$\frac{1}{2^1} = \frac{1}{2}$	$\frac{1}{2}$
2	$\frac{1}{2^2} = \frac{1}{4}$	$\frac{3}{4}$
3	$\frac{1}{2^4} = \frac{1}{8}$	$\frac{7}{8}$
4	$\frac{1}{2^4} = \frac{1}{16}$	$\frac{15}{16}$

You can see that the denominator of the sum is always equal to 2^n, and the numerator is always one less than that. Thus, the pattern for the running sum through n terms is:

$$\text{Running sum} = \frac{2^n - 1}{2^n}$$

Substituting 10 for n and splitting the numerator into two fractions yields choice (A).

16. **(C):** In terms of positive integers satisfying the inequality, only the following integers work: {5, 6, 7, 8}. Thus, 4 positive integers satisfy the inequality.

Similarly, only the following negative integers satisfy the inequality: {−5, −6, −7, −8}. Thus, 4 negative integers satisfy the inequality.

In total, there are 8 integers in A. The smallest integer is −8, which has an absolute value of 8, so **the two quantities are equal**.

17. **(A):** Since x and y are both positive integers, $x + y$ is positive and also $|x + y| = x + y$. Likewise, the absolute value signs in Quantity B have no effect, so $|x| − |y| = x − y$. Subtract x from both quantities and compare the remainders. In Quantity A, y is positive. In Quantity B, $−y$ is negative. Thus, **Quantity A is greater**.

18. **−10:** You can convert the averages to sums by simply multiplying the average by the number of terms in each expression given. Thus, $x + y = (2) \times 40 = 80$, $y + z = (2) \times 60 = 120$, and $x + y + z = (3) \times 30 = 90$.

The easiest way to solve this system of 3 variables and 3 equations is to subtract the first equation from the last, eliminating x and y immediately and giving you a value for z:

$$
\begin{array}{rl}
x + y + z = & 90 \\
- \ (x + y) \ \ \ \ \ = & -80 \\
\hline
z = & 10
\end{array}
$$

Plugging this value into the second equation, you see $y + 10 = 120$, so $y = 110$; plugging into the first equation, $x + 110 = 80$, so $x = −30$.

Thus, $x + z = (−30) + 10 = −20$, and the average of x and $z = −10$.

Note that you could also have started by subtracting the second equation from the last equation, solving first for x and then using that value to find y and z.

7

19. **(A) and (C):** Perhaps the easiest way to solve this problem is to pick numbers and see which combinations of pickles and onions cost the same amount. Since onions cost 3 times as much as pickles, try $6 for the cost of an onion and $2 for the cost of a pickle. Furthermore, use N for the cost of an onion purchased and P for the cost of a pickle.

Choice (A) translates to $9N + 3P = 9(\$6) + 3(\$2) = \$60$.

Choice (B) translates to $7N + 5P = 7(\$6) + 5(\$2) = \$52$.

Choice (C) translates to $7N + 9P = 7(\$6) + 9(\$2) = \$60$.

Choice (D) translates to $5N + 12P = 5(\$6) + 12(\$2) = \$54$.

Choice (E) translates to $5N + 14P = 5(\$6) + 14(\$2) = \$58$.

Therefore, **choices (A) and (C) are equal**.

20. **6:** When solving a quadratic equation, you must factor the original quadratic expression such that the constant terms in the two factors sum to the value of the coefficient in the x term (in this case, -10):

$$(x - 4)(x + ?) = 0$$

In this case, (-4) and "?" must sum to -10, so "?" must equal -6. Therefore, the other solution is $x = 6$.

Note that plugging 4 in for x in the original equation yields a value of -11 for k:

$$(4)^2 - 10(4) + 13 = k$$
$$16 - 40 + 13 = k$$
$$-11 = k$$

To verify, plug in 6 for x in the equation and see that it, too, produces a value of -11 for k:

$$(6)^2 - 10(6) + 13 = k$$
$$36 - 60 + 13 = k$$
$$-11 = k$$

Hard Practice Question Set

CAUTION: These problems are *very difficult*—more difficult than many of the problems you will likely see on the GRE. Consider these "Challenge Problems." Have fun!

1. $f(x) = x^2 + 1$. For which values of x does $f(x) = f\left(\dfrac{1}{x}\right)$?

Indicate <u>all</u> such values:

  [A] -2
  [B] -1
  [C] $-\dfrac{1}{2}$

  [D] $\dfrac{1}{2}$

  [E] 1
  [F] 2

2. If $x^3 + 3x^2 - 10x = 0$, indicate <u>all</u> the possible values for the sum of any <u>two</u> solutions for x.

Indicate <u>all</u> that apply.

  [A] -10
  [B] -5
  [C] -3
  [D] -2
  [E] 0
  [F] 2
  [G] 3

3. Each number S_N in a sequence can be expressed as a function of the preceding number (S_{N-1}) as follows: $S_N = \dfrac{2}{3} S_{N-1} - 4$. Which of the following equations correctly expresses the value of S_N in this sequence in terms of S_{N+2}?

  (A) $S_N = \dfrac{9}{4} S_{N+2} + 18$

  (B) $S_N = \dfrac{4}{9} S_{N+2} + 15$

  (C) $S_N = \dfrac{9}{4} S_{N+2} + 15$

  (D) $S_N = \dfrac{4}{9} S_{N+2} - 8$

  (E) $S_N = \dfrac{2}{3} S_{N+2} - 8$

7

4. If $a > 0$ and $b < 0$, which of the following statements are true about the values of x that solve the equation $x^2 - ax + b = 0$?

Indicate <u>all</u> such statements.

[A] They have opposite signs.
[B] Their sum is greater than zero.
[C] Their product equals $-b$.

5. If $r > 0$, $s \neq \dfrac{1}{2}$ and $r = \dfrac{3s+1}{1-2s}$, then $s =$

(A) $\dfrac{3r}{12+6r}$

(B) $-\dfrac{2r}{3}$

(C) $\dfrac{r-1}{3+2r}$

(D) $\dfrac{2}{3}(1-r)$

(E) $\dfrac{-1+r}{3}$

6.   **Quantity A**   **Quantity B**

            $x(4-x)$ 6

7. n is an integer, and $|2n+7| \leq 10$.

            Quantity A   **Quantity B**

The difference between the greatest and least   10
           possible values of n

8. $s^2 + t^2 < 1 - 2st$

            Quantity A   **Quantity B**
              $1 - s$ t

9. In a sequence a_1, a_2, ..., each term after the first is found by taking the negative of the preceding term, and adding 1. If $a_1 = 2$, what is the sum of the first 99 terms?

    (A) 49
    (B) 50
    (C) 51
    (D) 99
    (E) 101

10. The cost of shipping a purchase is s dollars up to a purchase value of p dollars, plus an additional 5% of any excess of the purchase price over p dollars. If the value of a purchase is x dollars (where $x > p$), what is the cost (in dollars) of shipping the purchase?

    (A) $s + 0.05x$
    (B) $s + 0.05p$
    (C) $0.05(s - p + x)$
    (D) $s + 0.05(x - p)$
    (E) $s + 0.05(p - x)$

11. Caleb and Dan play a game in which the loser of each round gives one half of his marbles to the other player. They start out with $4C$ and $4D$ marbles, respectively. If Caleb wins the first round and Dan wins the second round, how many marbles does Dan have at the end of the second round?

    (A) $2D$
    (B) $2C + D$
    (C) $2D + C$
    (D) $3D + C$
    (E) $3D + 2C$

7

12. Which of the following is the graph of the functional relationship $\frac{1}{2}(y-1)=|x-4|$?

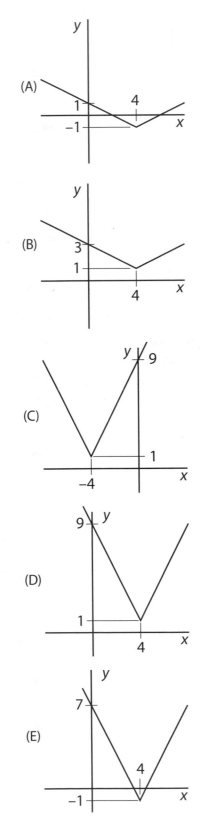

MANHATTAN
PREP

13. The stiffness of a diving board is proportional to the cube of its thickness and inversely proportional to the cube of its length. If diving board A is twice as long as diving board B and has 8 times the stiffness of diving board B, what is the ratio of the thickness of diving board A to that of diving board B? (Assume that the diving boards are equal in all respects other than thickness and length.)

14.
$$a = 5b^2 - 10b + 7$$

Quantity A	**Quantity B**
a	b

15.

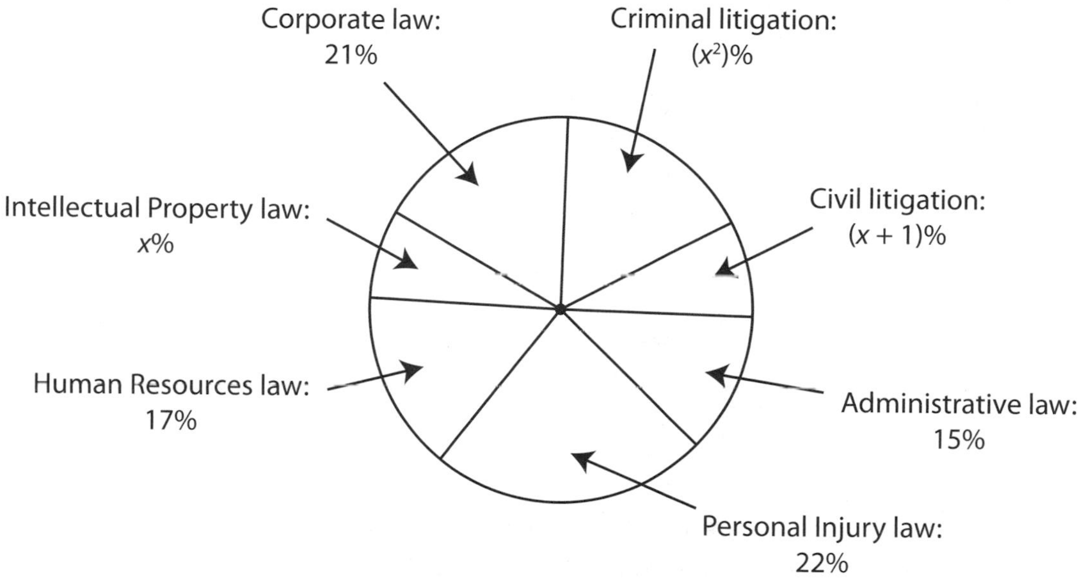

Corporate law: 21%

Criminal litigation: $(x^2)\%$

Intellectual Property law: $x\%$

Civil litigation: $(x + 1)\%$

Human Resources law: 17%

Administrative law: 15%

Personal Injury law: 22%

The circle graph above represents the type of law practiced by 55,000 members of an international law organization. The percent represented are exact.

Quantity A	**Quantity B**
The number of lawyers in the organization who practice *all* types of litigation	The number of lawyers who practice corporate law

7

16. If $|2z| - 1 \geq 2$, which of the following graphs could be a number line representing all the possible values of z?

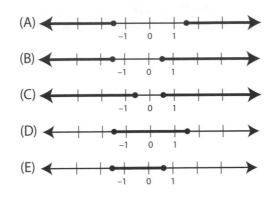

(A)
(B)
(C)
(D)
(E)

17. If $a - b = 16$ and $\sqrt{a} + \sqrt{b} = 8$, what is the value of $\sqrt{ab}$?

(A) 2
(B) 4
(C) 8
(D) 12
(E) 15

18.

$$\frac{2}{d} = \frac{2-d}{d-2}$$

Quantity A	**Quantity B**
d	0

19. The integer a is greater than 1 and is <u>not</u> equal to the square of an integer. Which of the following answer choices could <u>potentially</u> be equal to the square of an integer?

Indicate <u>all</u> that apply.

A $\sqrt{a}$
B $a^2 - 1$
C $a^2 + 1$
D $a^2 - a$
E $a^2 - 2a + 1$
F $2a$

20. If $a = b \times c^2$ and c decreases by 20% while a remains constant, by what percent does b increase?

Round your answer to the nearest 0.1%: ☐ %

Hard Practice Question Solutions

1. **(B) and (E):** If $f(x) = x^2 + 1$, then $f\left(\dfrac{1}{x}\right)$ can be written as $f\left(\dfrac{1}{x}\right) = \left(\dfrac{1}{x}\right)^2 + 1$, where you have simply substituted $\dfrac{1}{x}$ for x. Setting these two equations equal yields:

$$x^2 + 1 = \left(\frac{1}{x}\right)^2 + 1$$
$$x^2 = \frac{1}{x^2}$$
$$x^4 = 1$$

Thus, the only two solutions to this equation are $x = 1$ and $x = -1$.

If you have a problem seeing that the only two solutions are 1 and −1, you can continue the algebra and factor the above equation as follows:

$$x^4 - 1 = 0$$
$$(x^2 + 1)(x^2 - 1) = 0$$
$$(x^2 + 1)(x - 1)(x + 1) = 0$$

Where $x^2 + 1$ yields no real solutions, so the only solutions are given by $x = 1$ and $x = -1$.

Alternatively, you may simply take the answers and plug them into the problem. For example, using choice (A), $x = -2$, you find that $f(x) = f(-2) = (-2)^2 + 1 = 5$. Using the same value for x, you find that $\dfrac{1}{x} = -\dfrac{1}{2}$, which gives $f\left(\dfrac{1}{x}\right) = f\left(-\dfrac{1}{2}\right) = \left(-\dfrac{1}{2}\right)^2 + 1 = \dfrac{5}{4}$. Since $\dfrac{5}{4}$ is not equal to 5, you know that $f(x) = f\left(\dfrac{1}{x}\right)$ when $x = -2$. The same logic can be used to test each of the choices, and only $x = 1$ and $x = -1$ (choices (B) and (E)) satisfy the equality.

2. **(B), (C), and (F):** The cubic expression factors into x times a quadratic expression: $x(x^2 + 3x - 10)$, which further factors into $x(x + 5)(x - 2)$. Thus, $x(x + 5)(x - 2) = 0$ and $x = 0, -5$, or 2. Therefore, the sum of any *two* solutions for x could be any of:

$$0 + (-5) = -5$$
$$(-5) + 2 = -3$$
$$0 + 2 = 2$$

3. **(C):** The equation that describes the relationship between S_N and S_{N-1} also describes the relationship between S_{N+1} and S_N. Therefore, you can write $S_{N+1} = \dfrac{2}{3}S_N - 4$. Similarly, you can write $S_{N+2} = \dfrac{2}{3}S_{N+1} - 4$. Substituting for S_{N+1} in this equation, you get the following:

$$S_{N+2} = \frac{2}{3}\left(\frac{2}{3}S_N - 4\right) - 4$$

7

Solving for S_N in terms of S_{N+2}, you get:

$$S_{N+2} = \frac{4}{9}S_N - \frac{8}{3} - 4$$

$$\frac{4}{9}S_N = S_{N+2} + \frac{8}{3} + 4 = S_{N+2} + \frac{20}{3}$$

$$S_N = \frac{9}{4}S_{N+2} + 15$$

This equals choice (C).

4. **(A) and (B):** To gain some insight, first look at a few representative cases:

Case 1: Both solutions are positive. Example: $(x - 1)(x - 2) = 0$ or $x^2 - 3x + 2 = 0$.

Case 2: Both solutions are negative. Example: $(x + 1)(x + 2) = 0$ or $x^2 + 3x + 2 = 0$

Case 3: One solution is positive, the other is negative. Example: $(x + 1)(x - 2) = 0$ or $x^2 - x - 2 = 0$.

These examples show that the constant term at the end is positive whenever the two solutions are of the same sign. However, in the given equation, the constant equals b, which is less than 0. Thus, the two solutions must be of opposite signs, so choice (A) is correct. You can also see that the constant term equals the product of the two solutions. In this case, that product is negative, so choice (C) is incorrect.

Finally, the coefficient of the x term (i.e., the number that multiplies x in the given equation) is the *negative* of the sum of the two solutions. For example, in Case 1, the solutions are $+1$ and $+2$, which sum to $+3$, but the coefficient of x is -3. In the given equation, the coefficient of x equals $-a$, which is negative. Thus, choice (B) is correct: the sum of the two solutions must be positive.

5. **(C):** First, eliminate the fraction by multiplying both sides by $(1 - 2s)$:

$$r(1 - 2s) = 3s + 1$$
$$r - 2sr = 3s + 1$$

Next, since you are solving for s, you must collect s terms on one side: $r - 1 = 3s + 2rs$. Factor out s in order to isolate it: $r - 1 = s(3 + 2r)$. Finally, divide by $(3 + 2r)$ to arrive at $s = \dfrac{r-1}{3+2r}$. There is an alternative to this algebraic approach: picking numbers. Suppose you let $s = 3$. (In general, you want to avoid choosing 0 or 1 for variables, because those values can lead to unusual results and often similar results across the choices.) For that value of s, you find that $r = \dfrac{10}{(1-6)} = -2$. You would then substitute this value of r into each of the choices to determine which one gives you $s = 2$. Only choice (C) does.

6. **(B):** Expand Quantity A and subtract that quantity from both quantities in order to obtain a full quadratic expression in Quantity B:

$$4x - x^2$$
$$0$$

$$6$$
$$x^2 - 4x + 6$$

At this point, you can try to factor the resulting quadratic, but no simple factoring is apparent. The next option is to "complete the square," which is to manipulate the quadratic in Quantity B so that it includes the square of an expression:

$$0$$
$$0$$

$$(x^2 - 4x + 4) + 2$$
$$(x - 2)^2 + 2$$

As you can see, no matter what value you pick for x, the expression in Quantity B will never be less than 2 (because the squared term can never be negative). Thus, **Quantity B is greater.**

Another approach would be to test various values for x. For instance, starting from $x = 0$ and going up one integer at a time, you would see that $x(4 - x)$ increases until it reaches a maximum value of 4 (when $x = 2$), and then decreases again, indicating that it will always be less than 6. (To verify this, you can test $x = 1.5$ and $x = 2.5$ and demonstrate that the results are less than 4.)

A final option (which requires some insight into the graph of a quadratic function) is to recognize that the value of x for which the quadratic expression will be at an extreme (maximum or minimum) will be exactly halfway between the two roots, or solutions, of the quadratic. In this case, the roots of $x(4 - x) = 0$ are $x = 0$ and $x = 4$. Therefore, the extreme value is obtained when $x = 2$: $2 \times (4 - 2) = 4$, which is less than 6.

7. **(B):** The given inequality can also be written as follows: $-10 \le 2n + 7 \le 10$. Subtracting 7 from each term (*including* the middle term) yields $-17 \le 2n \le 3$. Finally, dividing all three terms by 2, you obtain $-8.5 \le n \le 1.5$. This is a range of 10. However, you must remember that n *has to be* an integer. Therefore, the greatest possible value of n is 1, and the least possible value of n is -8:

$$1 - (-8) = 9$$

$$10$$

Thus, **Quantity B is greater.**

8. **(A):** Manipulate the given inequality to get the s and t terms on one side of the inequality. In so doing, you can recognize the left-hand side of the inequality as one of the "special products":

$$s^2 + t^2 + 2st < 1$$
$$(s + t)^2 < 1$$

If the square of $(s + t)$ is less than 1, then $(s + t)$ itself must be between -1 and 1: $-1 < s + t < 1$. Subtracting s from all three terms yields: $-1 - s < t < 1 - s$. Therefore, t must be less than $1 - s$, and **Quantity A is greater.**

9. **(C):** Calculate the first few terms of the sequence using the definition $a_n = -a_{n-1} + 1$:

$$a_2 = -a_1 + 1 = -2 + 1 = -1$$
$$a_3 = -a_2 + 1 = -(-1) + 1 = 1 + 1 = 2$$

You can see that the sequence will now settle into a constant pattern: each pair of numbers will be 2 (when the item index is odd) and −1 (when the item index is even), with the sum of each pair equaling 1. There are 49 pairs in the first 98 terms, so the sum of the first 98 terms is 49. You can find the sum of the first 99 terms by adding the 99th term, which will be 2. Thus, the sum of the first 99 terms is 49 + 2 = 51.

10. **(D):** One approach is to do the problem algebraically. The amount by which the purchase price exceeds p dollars is given by $(x - p)$. The shipping cost will equal the fixed cost of s dollars, plus 5% of this excess amount: $s + 0.05(x - p)$.

Alternatively, you could pick numbers and calculate a target value. Suppose $s = 3$, $p = 5$, and $x = 7$. The shipping charges should equal $3 plus 5% of the difference of $7 and $5, which is $0.10. The target value is therefore $3.10. Substituting your values for s, p, and x into the answer choices indicates that the expression in choice (D) is correct.

11. **(E):** You can set up a table to track the progress of the game:

Round	Caleb's marbles	Dan's marbles
Start	$4C$	$4D$
After 1st (Caleb wins)	$4C + \dfrac{4D}{2} = 4C + 2D$	$\dfrac{4D}{2} = 2D$
After 2nd (Dan wins)	$\dfrac{4C + 2D}{2} = 2C + D$	$2D + (2C + D) = 3D + 2C$

Thus, **choice (E) is the correct answer.**

You could, alternatively, pick numbers for C and D and track the progress of the game and then test each of the choices to see which leads to the correct answer.

12. **(D):** The functional relationship can be rewritten as $y = 2|x - 4| + 1$. The "notch" of the absolute value function will be located at the value of x for which the absolute value reaches the minimum possible value of 0. That will occur when $x = 4$. The value of y will then equal $2|0| + 1 = 1$. Also, when $x = 0$, y will equal $2|-4| + 1 = 9$. This relationship is depicted in choice (D).

13. **4:** You can pick some numbers to make the problem easier. With the given information, the general formula for a diving board's stiffness is $S = K\dfrac{T^3}{L^3}$, where T is thickness, L is length, and k is some constant. Suppose diving board A has thickness equal to 4 and length equal to 2. Then, its stiffness would equal $k\dfrac{4^3}{2^3} = \dfrac{64}{8}k = 8k$.

MANHATTAN
PREP

To simplify matters further, suppose $k = 1$ (normally you would not use 1 when picking numbers, but because k is not relevant for solving the problem—it will cancel out when you do the math—you pick 1 for simplicity). The stiffness of diving board A is then $S_A = 8$.

You are told that diving board B is half the length of diving board A, and also has $\dfrac{1}{8}$ the stiffness, of diving board A. This means that the length of diving board B is 1 and its stiffness equals 1. Denote the thickness of diving board B with T. You can then write (again assuming $k = 1$ for simplicity, again noting that the same value of k must apply to both diving boards because they are equal in all other respects):

$$S_B = 1 = \frac{T^3}{1^3}$$

From this, you can determine that $T^3 = 1$ and $T = 1$. The ratio of the thickness of diving board A to that of diving board B must therefore equal $4/1 = 4$.

14. **(A):** You can try to factor the quadratic given in the problem, but no simple factoring is apparent. The next option is to "complete the square," which is to manipulate the quadratic in Quantity A so that it includes the square of an expression:

$5(b^2 - 2b) + 7$	b
$5(b^2 - 2b + 1) + 7 - 5(1)$	b
$5(b - 1)^2 + 2$	b

It's clearer to see the answer if you subtract b and 2 from both sides next:

$5(b - 1)^2 - b$	-2

The minimum value for the expression in Quantity A is -1 when $b = 1$. Clearly, as b moves farther away from 1 in the positive direction, eventually the term $5(b - 1)^2$ will rise faster than $-b$ falls. And as b falls, $-b$ will rise, so both terms in Quantity A will increase. Therefore, you only need to test a few values just greater than $b = 1$ to see what happens to Quantity A (it will be useful to use the Calculator here):

b	$5(b - 1)^2 - b$	-2
1	-1	-2
1.01	-1.0095	-2
1.05	-1.0375	-2
1.1	-1.05	-2
1.11	-1.0495	-2

Therefore, the minimum for Quantity A appears to be approximately -1.05 and Quantity A will always be greater than Quantity B. (Indeed, the minimum for Quantity A occurs when $b = 1.1$.)

15. **(C):** The only types of lawyers listed in the graph who practice litigation are Criminal Litigation and Civil Litigation lawyers. The percent of the lawyers who practice litigation is thus represented by $x^2 + (x + 1)$, and the percent of lawyers who practice Corporate law is 21%. (For the purposes of this problem, you can ignore "number" of lawyers vs. "percent," because the problem specifies that the percent represented are exact.)

Because all the pieces of the circle graph must sum to 100%, you can write an equation and solve for x, starting with the upper-left segment and working clockwise:

$$21 + x^2 + (x + 1) + 15 + 22 + 17 + x = 100$$

$$x^2 + 2x + 76 = 100$$

$$x^2 + 2x - 24 = 0$$

$$(x + 6)(x - 4) = 0 \qquad \rightarrow \qquad x = 4 \text{ or } -6$$

Since a circle graph cannot contain a "negative" segment, x must equal 4. Therefore, the percent of the organization that works in litigation equals $4^2 + (4 + 1) = 21$, which is equal to the percent that works in Corporate law. Thus, **the two quantities are equal**.

16. **(A):** The first step is to isolate the absolute value expression: $|2z| - 1 \geq 2$, so $|2z| \geq 3$. Therefore, $2z \leq -3$ or $2z \geq 3$. Dividing both inequalities by 2, you get $z \leq -1.5$ or $z \geq 1.5$. Only choice (A) displays a graph for which the relevant range correctly does not include −1, 0, or 1, and includes values above 1 and below −1.

17. **(E):** The efficient approach to this problem is to recognize that this problem can be solved using a variant of the *difference of squares* special product: $(a + b)(a - b) = a^2 - b^2$. The distinction is that each of the exponents in this expression is halved in this problem (remember, $x^{1/2} = \sqrt{x}$). Thus, you can use:

$$\left(\sqrt{a} + \sqrt{b}\right)\left(\sqrt{a} - \sqrt{b}\right) = a - b = 16$$

Since the first expression equals 8, you know that the second expression must equal $\dfrac{16}{8} = 2$.

Next, you can use the two equations containing square root expressions, and eliminate the $\sqrt{b}$ terms by adding the two equations together:

$$\begin{array}{r} \sqrt{a} + \sqrt{b} = 8 \\ + \ \sqrt{a} - \sqrt{b} = 2 \\ \hline 2\sqrt{a} \qquad = 10 \end{array}$$

Alternative explanation:

$$x = \sqrt{a}$$
$$y = \sqrt{b}$$
so given
$$x^2 - y^2 = 16$$
$$x + y = 8$$

What is $\sqrt{ab}$? $\rightarrow$ what is xy?

Therefore, $\sqrt{a} = 5$ and $a = 25$. Plugging this into the first equation, you get $b = 9$ and $ab = 225$. Thus, $\sqrt{ab} = 15$.

Note that solving this question is much more difficult if the special product is not employed—one would have to first isolate one of the radicals, square both sides, employ substitution, isolate the radical again, square both sides, etc.

MANHATTAN
PREP

18. **(B):** From the original equation, you can cross-multiply to arrive at:

$$(d)(d-2)\frac{2}{d} = \frac{2-d}{d-2}(d)(d-2)$$
$$2d - 4 = 2d - d^2$$
$$-4 = -d^2$$
$$d^2 = 4$$

It would appear at first glance that d could equal 2 or −2. However, remember that in the original equation, $(d-2)$ appeared in a denominator. Therefore, 2 is not a solution, as it would result in a 0 appearing in a denominator, which is undefined (actually, indeterminate, as the numerator would also equal 0).

Only −2 is a possible solution to the equation, and **Quantity B is therefore greater.**

19. **(E) and (F):** Since a is not the square of an integer, its square root cannot possibly be the square of an integer (in fact, the square root of a cannot even be an integer itself, since a is not a perfect square). This rules out choice (A).

Choices (B) and (C) can be eliminated by the following logic: if a is greater than 1, a^2 will be at least 4. Additionally, since a is an integer, a^2 will be a perfect square. There are no different perfect squares that are one unit apart (other than 0 and 1), so $a^2 + 1$ and $a^2 - 1$ cannot possibly be perfect squares (they are each one unit away from a perfect square that cannot be 0 or 1).

Choice (D) can be eliminated for a similar reason. If $a = 2$, then $a^2 = 4$, and the nearest lower perfect square is 1, 3 units away (3 is greater than 2). If $a = 3$, then $a^2 = 9$, and the nearest lower perfect square is 4, 5 units away (5 is greater than 3). If $a = 4$, then $a^2 = 16$, and the nearest lower perfect square is 9, 7 units away (7 is greater than 4). This pattern shows that subtracting a from a^2 will result in a number somewhere in between a^2, a perfect square, and the next lower perfect square, which is $(a-1)^2$.

Choice (E) *must* be a perfect square, because the expression can be factored as $(a-1)^2$. Since a is an integer, $a - 1$ is an integer and $(a-1)^2$ is a perfect square.

Finally, choice (F) can be a perfect square whenever a is equal to half of a perfect square. For example, if $a = 2$ or 8, then $2a = 4$ or 16, respectively—both of which are perfect squares.

20. **56.3:** If c decreases by 20%, then the right-hand side of the equation changes by a factor of 0.64. To come to this conclusion, create a new variable, B, to represent the new value of b after the decrease in c:

$$a = b \times c^2 = B \times (c - 0.2c)^2 = B \times (0.8c)^2 = 0.64Bc^2$$

The ratio of B to b is thus:

$$bc^2 = 0.64Bc^2$$

$$\frac{B}{b} = \frac{1}{0.64} = 1.5625$$

Therefore, b must change by a factor of 1.5625, or a 56.25% increase. Rounded to the nearest 0.1 percentage point, the percent change in b will be 56.3.

STUDY ANYWHERE!

WITH MANHATTAN PREP'S GRE FLASH CARDS

coterie

(noun)

COH-ter-ee

587

Definition: Close or exclusive group, clique

Usage: The pop star never traveled anywhere without a **coterie** of assistants and managers.

Related Words: *Cabal* (conspiracy, group of people who plot), *Entourage* (group of attendants)

More Info: In French, a *coterie* was a group of tenant farmers.

With our flashcards you can study both math and verbal concepts on the go!

Both our 500 Essential Words and a 500 Advanced Words cards go above and beyond providing abstract, out-of-context definitions. Complete with definitions, example sentences, pronunciations, and related words, this two-volume set comprises the most comprehensive vocabulary study tool on the market.

Our GRE Math Flash Cards provide practical exposure to the basic math concepts tested on the GRE.

Designed to be user-friendly for all students, these cards include easy-to-follow explanations of math concepts that promise to enhance comprehension and build fundamental skills.

For the revised GRE

M

MANHATTAN PREP

GRE® FLASH CARDS

500 Math Flash Cards

✓ Designed specifically for the math question types found on the revised GRE

✓ Cards cover all tested content and include clear, efficient explanations

✓ Want Verbal? Check out our flash card sets *500 Essential Words* & *500 Advanced Words*

*GRE is a registered trademark of the Educational Testing Service (ETS), which neither sponsors nor endorses this test product.